Messages of Hope

The Metaphysical Memoir of a Most Unexpected Medium

Suzanne Giesemann

www.OneMindBooks.com

Cover design by Rob Johnson, www.toprotype.com
Interior design by Linda Morehouse, www.WeBuildBooks.com
Production assistance by Elisabeth Giesemann

Library of Congress Control Number: 2011915859
Library of Congress Cataloging-in-Publication Data
    Messages of Hope : The Metaphysical Memoir of a Most
    Unexpected Medium/Suzanne Giesemann

ISBN: 978-0-9838539-1-6

Printed in the United States of America
First Edition

Published by One Mind Books: www.OneMindBooks.com

To all of my angels—

You know who you are.

Also by Suzanne Giesemann:

Conquer Your Cravings
Living a Dream
It's Your Boat Too
The Priest and the Medium
Love Beyond Words

Co-Authored with Janet Nohavec:

Through the Darkness
Where Two Worlds Meet

Acknowledgments

This is a book I wish I'd never had to write. The major changes in my life that are recounted here are the result of tremendous loss for my family. I would give anything to change the defining event of this story, but life doesn't work like that. We come here to learn certain life lessons, and some of them are learned the hard way. When faced with such turning points, the option is to curl up into a ball, or to make something good come of tragedy. I have dedicated my life to the latter, and this book is one way of doing that. The goal of *Messages of Hope* is not to tell my story, but to share the universal life lessons and Truths of the Spirit that I hope will shine through this story.

One of the things I learned as my life spun off into unforeseen directions is how incredibly interconnected we all are. No project is ever the work of one individual. Every person who is mentioned in this book holds a special place in my heart. You are all messengers, and I thank you.

Hidden behind the scenes, but no less special, are the members of my "heart circle," my agent, Bill Hammond, and a true angel, Linda Morehouse.

A special thank you to Ann and Chris Lavelle for understanding the importance of the message.

Finally, I thank my husband, Ty, who I love beyond words. He did not sign up to be married to a medium. Regardless, he has walked beside me every step of this unexpected journey, always giving me his full love and support. As a result, he has learned that lightworkers do not belong to the electricians' union, and he continues to bring light into every moment of my life.

Messages of Hope

Contents

Introduction

I heard the words in my head. Eyes closed, pad of paper in my lap, I wrote the sentences as they came to me. They were beautiful, no doubt about it. Yet still the thought nagged me: *I'm making this up.*

I didn't want to discount what I was hearing, so I kept my pen poised, especially after the conversation I'd had the night before. I'd traveled to Massachusetts to give a presentation on mediumship at a metaphysical center. Nancy Gratta, the center's owner, pulled me aside afterwards and told me that her guides had been speaking to her during my talk.

Back then, I still had my doubts about the whole spirit guide thing. The spirit world was real—this I knew from my experiences as a budding medium—but *guides*? I'd started feeling a familiar presence during my meditation, but whoever "it" or "they" were, they hadn't yet chosen to identify themselves.

Those who'd been dealing with the spirit world far longer than I had were forever talking about their guides as if they knew them. The former Navy officer in me always wanted to ask, *Where's the evidence*? Luckily, the seeker in me allowed for possibilities beyond that which I could prove, so I smiled at Nancy and said, "Oh, yeah? What did they tell you?"

"You're going to receive understanding this week in your meditation," she said. "You'll receive guidance in preparation for your talk next week."

"What kind of guidance?" I asked, suddenly worried that this was Nancy's polite way of telling me I had some more work to do.

"They didn't say," she said. "I just know it's going to be a wonderful experience, and I'm excited for you." She added that I should ask for clarification about judgment in the afterlife—a subject that had come up during the question-and-answer session that evening. I felt that I'd stumbled a bit with my answer, as I had no first-hand knowledge of the topic, and now I winced. Either Nancy or her guides were pretty perceptive.

With Nancy's advice still fresh in my mind the next morning, I prepared to meditate. My husband and I were cruising aboard our sailboat for the summer. No matter what our plans for the day, Ty respected my need to retreat to the aft cabin for half an hour of privacy each morning before heading for a new port.

With Ty reading in the forward cabin, I pulled a pad of paper and pen from a drawer and laid them on the desk before me. My mentor, Janet, one of the best mediums I knew, had been telling me for the past month to have pen and paper nearby as I meditated. She felt that I would be doing automatic writing as part of my mediumistic development.

I'd asked Janet if the spirits would move my pen, or if I'd just hear their words and write them down. She said it would be the latter, but that I'd know they weren't my words. I'd tried it a few times, and twice had some beautiful, spiritual insights come to me, but each time I felt they were my own thoughts and not the words of spirit. Still, it didn't hurt to have the paper ready.

I sat back in the padded gray chair that was bolted to the deck and closed my eyes. The gentle rocking of the boat helped me to relax and quiet my mind. Having meditated daily for three years, I easily slipped into a light altered state.

I began, as always, with my prayers, giving gratitude to God for life and its many blessings and stating my intent to be of service. Remembering Nancy's advice, I asked for greater understanding and guidance about the subject of judgment and about my upcoming presentation. Then, as I'd learned to do when giving a mediumistic reading, I made the switch from active thought to passive, receptive mode, and I waited.

It came to me shortly thereafter: the lightheadedness I'd come to recognize as the unmistakable presence of spirit. Spirit's vibration is much higher than ours, and whenever its energy blended with mine, my head would initially spin. It wasn't an unpleasant sensation, and I smiled. For me, the dizziness was evidential in itself, and I welcomed it.

Moments later I felt a subtle, inexplicable urge to pick up the pen and paper. Without opening my eyes, I reached out and picked them up. I laid the pad in my lap and sat with the pen poised to write.

As above, so below.

I heard the words as clearly as if they'd been spoken aloud. They came to me just as they did in a reading when a client's loved one in spirit would plant thoughts in my mind.

Eyes still closed, I wrote the words at the top of the page, then started a new line with the words I heard next:

You reap what you sow.

I recognized a direct answer to my question on judgment, but found nothing I didn't already know in the message. Fascinated, but still convinced I was simply talking to myself, I listened for more.

Judge not others, but of yourself be the judge.

The words made sense, but still I doubted the source.

Then: *You, in your heart, know the truth: Happiness is earned; let others not be spurned.*

I wrote the words verbatim, moving my hand by feel down the page, but something about the phrases tickled my awareness.

As above, so below.

You reap what you sow . . .

Earned . . .

Spurned . . .

Then I got it. These weren't just random thoughts; these words were *rhyming*! I knew the goal of meditation was to keep my mind empty, but I couldn't suppress a thought that was very clearly my own:

My God . . . they sent me a poet!

My mentor often stressed to me the intelligence of the spirit world, but this was downright brilliant. Whatever force was behind this new approach had figured out that I would never believe that anything I heard in meditation hadn't come from my own thoughts. So they had chosen the one mode of expression that I had always shied away from: poetry.

It's true that as an author and a speaker, words were my tools, but poetry was alien to me. With my black and white brain, honed from 20 years of military service, I'd always felt there was only one way to interpret poetry. If I didn't get it "right," then I had failed. So I stuck to prose. I had never studied poetry, never wrote it, and truth be told, never enjoyed reading it. I was the last person who would write in verse, yet there I sat, hearing and now obediently writing down line after rhyming line.

As the bottom of the page grazed my palm, and with eyes still closed, I turned to a new page as the speed of the transmission picked up. The words came as fast as I could write them, and I filled two more pages before they finally stopped.

I had three pages with rhyming words, but only a vague idea of their content. What I'd written slipped from my memory like a hazy dream before the ink could dry, yet I knew that what lay recorded on the paper held meaning. Overwhelmed, I laid down the pen, lowered my head into my hands, and quietly sobbed. Over the past three years the spirit world had repeatedly answered my prayers to prove their presence to me and to transform my life. That morning they did it in a new, wholly unexpected, and astonishing way.

I rose from the chair and moved unsteadily to the forward cabin with the notepad in hand. Ty looked up with concern from his seat at the dinette.

"Are you okay?" he asked. "I heard you crying."

I shook my head. "Something happened. I think I wrote a poem, but it didn't come from me." Sitting across from him, I turned to the first page of the pad. The lines crossed the paper at a slant. The writing was a bit unsteady, but for the most part, legible.

My husband seemed rightfully confused. "You think you wrote a poem?"

I nodded, still staring at the page. "I heard the words and I could tell they were rhyming, but just as fast as I wrote them I forgot them." I raised my eyes to his. "Can we read it together?"

"Of course."

The air seemed heavy, the anticipation palpable. I began reading aloud the phrases I'd first heard:

As above, so below.
You reap what you sow.

I read the other lines about judgment, explaining to Ty that this was in answer to a direct question I'd asked in prayer, then I continued reading, as if hearing the lines for the first time:

Yes, prepare,
But speak with confidence if you dare.
Ours is to leave you without care.
Such a gift is very rare.

I began to cry again as I recognized the answer to the second question about my upcoming presentation, just as Nancy's guides had predicted.

From love we come, it's in your genes.
You have the talent, we the means.
Rest in peace, assured of light.
With us beside you, you'll soar in flight.

The world is ready for these your words.
They wait and listen with wings like birds.
For ours is yours and yours is ours.
Such is the greatness of the Great Spirit's powers.

I glanced up at Ty. His face reflected the awe I felt. It became harder to read now as emotion constricted my throat.

Blessed are all who know these truths.
Shout it, blast it, from the roofs.
Be our voice, we work with you.
We come to speak of beauty true.

Divine is the light of which we speak.
Beauty lies in the watch we keep.
Speak of love, speak of beauty …
This, my dear, is your great duty.

We love you and hold you in our keep.
Go forth and trust that you can speak.
With this we leave you this blessed day.
Come back to us and together we'll pray.

For we are here; at your side we wait.
It's with great hope we anticipate
The truths you'll carry to those who listen.
The truths of God on your words will glisten.

Go now and rest, for there's work to do.
We have great love and trust in you.
You have our blessing. In you we're proud.
Take our wisdom and shout it loud.

We love you all. For this we've come.
There is no rest 'til the Spirit's work is done.

I laid the notepad in my lap and looked across at Ty. He appeared stunned, and I was filled with overwhelming emotion when I saw his red eyes and the tears on his cheeks.

He shook his head and said softly, "You weren't back there twenty minutes."

I found myself whispering the same as he. "I know, and I didn't start writing until more than halfway into my meditation, so all of that came to me in less than ten minutes."

Neither of us spoke for a long time, then Ty voiced my thoughts: "You couldn't have done that yourself."

And that's why I was crying. Ty knew as well as I did that I was no poet. He had patiently read the first drafts of the four nonfiction books I'd written and he knew the kind of books I liked to read. I wasn't a classics kind of gal. Poetry had never entered the equation.

If intelligent beings wanted to let me know that the words in my head were not my own, sending me beautiful thoughts with perfect rhyme and rhythm was a great way to get my attention. Nancy's parting words from the night before echoed in my ears: "They're going to give you such evidence."

Boy, had they ever.

The rest of the morning passed in a daze. My fingers didn't want to work as I typed the words of the poem into my computer. With the file now formatted and saved, I called my mentor to share the experience. Janet listened as I read the long poem. When finished, I waited for her reaction. There was no response. I pulled the phone from my ear and looked at the phone's screen, thinking I'd lost the connection. It appeared to be fine.

"Janet? Are you there?"

Another pause, then, "Yeah, I'm here. I'm just speechless."

Janet knew I was no poet. She had a friend who wrote poetry and had shared his verses with me in the past. At the time, I read a few and sheepishly admitted to her that I didn't really care for the genre. She hadn't forgotten that conversation, and now agreed with my assessment that the spirit world had pulled a good one.

I wasn't good for much of anything the rest of the day, other than sitting in the cockpit and staring out at the water as Ty did the sailing.

The next morning I sat to meditate, hoping I would have a similar experience as the day before. The spirits didn't disappoint me. Once I reached the peaceful altered state, the words flowed easily, giving me no time to think or critique. The poets seemed to sense that I needed their assurance, for they told me,

This is sacred work you do.
It's out of love we come to you.
Fear not that words will leave you dry.
We have the time, no need to try.

In fact, the few times I allowed my mind to get in the way, the words stopped. Only when I returned to the passive, receptive state and simply listened, did the poetry resume with the same easy flow:

Never doubt that we are here.
Think of us and we'll draw near.
For this is what we've come to do -
To share our thoughts with all of you.

Write them down as fast you will.
There's more to come, more wisdom still.
For this our work has just begun.
Relax, breathe deep and have some fun.

Thus began a daily voyage of discovery into the wonders and wisdom of the world beyond our physical senses. The poems came to me every day for just over a year, in periods of meditation. I merely took dictation, writing—as I had at the beginning, nonstop with pen in hand, paper in my lap—meaningful, multi-stanza verses in mere minutes. I always wrote with eyes closed, except for the one time the voice told me to open them and look. When I did, I saw that my pen had run out of ink.

They didn't want me to miss a word.

I never knew the theme of the day's poem until it came through. The rhythm, rhyming pattern, and voice changed frequently, yet always there was a comforting, loving message with the unifying thread of oneness. The first few poems held specific guidance for me, then the poetry took on a more universal tone, applicable to all.

The poems may never win a prize for their literary value, but those who read them tell me they have a special calming, healing effect. I know this is because they carry the energy of their Source.

I asked the poets one day what I should call them, and they answered, *The Council of Poets.* Then they added,

Yes, it is good . . . to know it.

Which goes to show you that you don't need a physical body to have a sense of humor.

Then I asked, "How many are you?" and heard:

Many are we in number
Ne'er to slumber
For the work that's planned
To bring to man
These Messages of Hope.

The poems have been an amazing source of spiritual wisdom for me and for those who read them. They answer such questions as, "Is this life all there is? What is my purpose, and is there really a God?" But do we all have access to inspiration and guidance beyond our present consciousness? I say yes. I don't just believe this is so; I *know* we do, for we are all manifestations of the One Divine Mind, of God. You may never be guided with poetic phrases, but whatever you need to know is there for the asking, with answers available to you in whatever way is most appropriate for you.

My story begins with the unanticipated journey that took me from Commander in the Navy, commanding officer, and aide-de-camp to the Chairman of the Joint Chiefs of Staff, to my current experiences as a psychic-medium and channel for the spirit world. In my former role, I flew on Air Force One with the President. I sat in on top-secret hearings on Capitol

Hill and at the Pentagon. I visited the White House Strategy Room and the Oval Office on official business. And today? Today I sit in a darkened room and talk to dead people.

So, okay, I may not fit the stereotype of a medium, and in a way, that's a good thing. People tell me my straight-laced background makes talking about the other side somehow more palatable to them. To that I say, "Whatever works." The evidence that this life is not all there is often comes to us in ways that we can never truly prove, so some folks get a little nervous discussing such things. Believe me, I didn't sit around with my Navy shipmates talking about the spirit world when I was on active duty.

Don't get me wrong; it wasn't a matter of "Don't ask, don't tell," but simply that I didn't realize I had the ability to contact the other side back then. It was, however, a bit like coming out of the closet as I got used to using the word "medium" when referring to myself.

The first time I shared some of the stories you'll read here with one of my former military colleagues was in a fancy restaurant outside Washington, D.C. I sat across the table from Mark "Ranger" Jones, the former senior enlisted aide to the Chairman of the Joint Chiefs. Always a mover and shaker, Ranger had risen from soldier in the Army to CEO of his own company, the Ranger Group. As I told my former sidekick about the spirit-inspired poetry and my mediumistic readings, his eyes grew ever wider.

Hesitant to say more, I leaned in and said, "Look, Ranger. You *know* me."

We had spent a lot of time together on our travels around the globe with General Shelton. We watched each other's backs and developed an abiding mutual respect.

Ranger laid his fork on his plate and studied me carefully. "Yes, ma'am," he replied after a nerve-wracking pause. "I *do* know you. And that's the only reason why right now I'm not saying, 'Waiter! Check, please!'"

As outlandish as the experiences I shared that day seemed to both of us, Ranger knew that I prided myself on my honesty and integrity. I was not one to embellish stories. These days I've received so much jaw-dropping evidence from the other side that I no longer hesitate to use the M-word when I tell people what I do.

Through the poetry and my readings, I've been given the answers to those big life questions I mentioned earlier, and I'm satisfied with them. They've come to me in rhyming verses from wise beings who seem to have figured out the things with which we mortals continue to struggle. I'll share some of those verses with you throughout these pages. If they touch your soul and make you see life in new ways, that's great. If, after reading these *Messages of Hope*, you continue on your personal journey to find the answers first-hand, all the better.

We come to this earth for one important reason: to develop our divinity—to kindle that loving spark of the Divine that lies within each of us. This earth is a great place of learning for us spirit-beings, and there is no shortage of lessons. When life is going great, you may not feel the need to ponder the really deep issues. That's the way it was with me, anyway. But the Universe has a way of making sure we learn the lessons we came here to learn.

A few years back my life took a sudden and unexpected turn down a road filled with nearly unbearable pain. From that place I discovered abilities I never dreamed I'd have, leaving me with a new sense of fulfillment, peace, and joy as I use those abilities to help others.

The same gifts await all who respond to the call of their spirit.

It's my hope that in reading this book, you, too, will discover a grander version of Reality than the one you were raised to accept. It's my hope that you'll find here the motivation to deepen your connection with your personal spirit and with the Great Spirit, and thus find the lasting peace and fulfillment that are your birthright.

Is wisdom available to all of us in the silence? The Council of Poets nod their heads and tell us:

Searching for answers
You need not look far.
The answers you seek
Are as close as you are.

For your Higher Self—
That which "spirit" you call
Is connected supremely
With the Source of it All.

Oh God—Source of All That Is—thank you for this gift of Life. Without the gift of Spirit, I could not even breathe. With Spirit, ALL things are possible.

Today I ask you and the spirit world to transform my life. Open my eyes that I may truly see why I am here and what it is I need to know. Guide me and show me how I may serve. Allow me to see and be only love and to appreciate the oneness of all life.

May I go forth today as the Spirit-being that I am, experiencing the fullness of all life and receiving Life in all its fullness in return. Help me to trust, to relax, and to see the perfection of Life as it is unfolding.

May I stay focused today on love, and may I bring comfort and light wherever I go.

Amen.

1

9/11—Up Close and Personal

On this day a group of men
Inflicted terror great and then
Sat back to laugh and brag and boast
Of acts of which they were the host.

It pains us greatly when some lose sight
Of the worth of man, of what is right,
When killing comes with equal ease
As the tiny effort it takes to breathe.

Understanding of this for most is hard—
To look at life with so little regard.
It's sickness they suffer as a whole.
This sickness starts within the soul …

Sick within my soul: that's how I felt as I peered through
the tiny window of our aircraft. I would have much rather
had my head buried under a pillow, instead of experiencing
this nightmare first-hand. Just a few thousand feet below, the
smoke billowed upward from what remained of the World
Trade Center towers. I knew I had a unique vantage point,
for the pilot had told me that all other aircraft in U.S. airspace
had been grounded by then.

An hour earlier I'd watched our aircrew open the safe and take out their authentication tables. I listened, incredulous, as they broadcast the coded information into the radio while we flew south to Washington. This was a scenario I'm sure they'd practiced many times, but this was no drill. Their transmissions that morning ensured that fighter jets wouldn't shoot down our plane. It was critical to get our special passenger back to the capital: my boss, the Chairman of the Joint Chiefs of Staff.

We'd borrowed the Air Force chief's jet for our flight to Europe, where later that week my general, the top-ranking officer in the United States armed forces, was to have been knighted by Queen Elizabeth. We were a couple of hours over the Atlantic when we got word about the terrorists' attack on New York. I put on a headset and spoke with a colonel back at our office in the Pentagon. As he filled me in on what he knew, I could hear a commotion in the background.

"Hang on a minute," the colonel told me. "Something just happened here. I think a bomb may have gone off."

Of course it wasn't a bomb. It was a jet slamming into the far side of the building that we'd just left that morning. Minutes later when my general gave me the nod, I went to the cockpit and told the pilot to take us back to Washington.

"Commander," he said, "Our flight path is going to take us right over Manhattan."

And that's how the handful of us on that aircraft became the only people in the country to see both the World Trade Center and the Pentagon with our own eyes on the very day of the attack. I wasn't alone, however, in feeling the shock and dismay of so many others that human beings could harbor such hate and disregard for their fellow man.

Within an hour of passing New York City, we landed at Andrews Air Force Base. The general's sedan and driver were

waiting, along with an unprecedented police escort of ten mo-
torcycles and three patrol cars to lead us back to Washington.
We were used to this kind of lights-and-sirens escort when we
visited foreign countries, but not in our own hometown.

All the way into the city the roads were eerily empty, save
for police cars parked at odd angles across random intersec-
tions. No one spoke as we sped across the Southeast-South-
west Freeway, usually jammed with cars at midday. Across
the Fourteenth Street Bridge, a heavy gray blanket hung in
the sky over Arlington. And there, to the right of the highway,
was the source of the thick smoke: our five-sided headquar-
ters. On fire.

We pulled up to the River Entrance, passing machine-
gun-toting soldiers in full battle dress. I followed the Chairman into the building where the acrid smoke assaulted my
nostrils, forever imprinting itself in my memory. The civilian
guards who normally greeted us with smiles watched with
grave faces as we made a beeline for the general's office.

After a brief update from his advisors, the Chairman
asked to be taken to see the scope of the damage to the Pentagon. Hearing this, I took a deep breath. Wherever the general
went, I went. Military officers were supposed to be tough, but
I felt anything but strong at that moment. Always sensitive,
I cringed at the thought of seeing devastation on such a large
scale.

We headed toward the Pentagon's inner courtyard, a
shortcut to the far side of the building. The hallways along
the way were dim and deserted, save for a few people wearing
surgical masks to filter the smoke. Cutting across the park-
like center of the Pentagon, I looked around at the odd scene.
Normally filled with people chatting, smoking, or grabbing a
bite to eat from the courtyard snack stand, the area was now
filled with medical personnel in surgical scrubs and soldiers

in camouflage uniforms. Many sat on the ground staring blankly ahead. Small, black plastic packages were laid out in neat rows on the grass, and I realized with a shudder that the bundles were empty body bags, ready for use.

I desperately wanted to turn back, my fight-or-flight syndrome on full alert. I was definitely not prepared to see body parts, but my job required that I stay with the Chairman.

Having crossed the courtyard, we entered the fifth corridor. Picturing the Pentagon's layout in my head, I knew the impact site was only a short distance ahead and to our left. The power was out here, and the smoke was thicker than ever. I held onto a colleague's belt loop as we groped our way into a pitch-black stairwell, thinking that we had no business walking into such a hazardous area.

Luckily, the Chairman's bodyguard must have had the same thought, for moments later he recommended we approach from the outside. Relief surged through me as we turned and made our way out the Mall Entrance into the welcome sunlight.

Rounding the corner of the building was like stepping onto the set of a disaster movie. A field of tents and rescue vehicles lay before us. Fire trucks parked on the sodden grass sprayed water onto the building's burning roof. Dozens of ambulances lined the sidewalk. As if in a dream, I stepped around a jagged chunk of a jet engine that lay in the grass, tragically out of place.

The focus of all the attention now lay directly before us: a gaping hole in a wall that had previously been just like the one outside our office. Now its exposed beams, broken windows, and blackened limestone created a painful portrait that my brain struggled to accept.

This was done on purpose?

Office interiors lay exposed like three-sided sets on a stage. I pictured the workers at their desks hours earlier, and prayed that most had gotten out. It was obvious that those unlucky enough to have been where now there was nothing but a huge void hadn't had a chance.

Emergency personnel scurried past us, nodding in respect to my four-star boss. Like the rest of us, the Chairman watched the rescue operation in silence and gravely shook his head. There was little to say.

We headed back into the building, where the Chairman's executive assistant informed me that the general needed to go to the National Military Command Center. The Vice-Chairman had been holed up there with the Joint Staff's top leadership since the morning. Now back in familiar territory, I led the way to the command post's main entrance where a security guard nodded us through.

With the general behind closed doors, I leaned on a counter next to a television and stared at the screen.

"You haven't seen this yet?" asked an Air Force officer who worked in the command center.

I shook my head.

"Keep watching. They'll show a clip of one of the planes actually flying into the second tower."

I watched in horror the scene I would later turn my head to avoid as the news media endlessly replayed it.

Only essential personnel were required to report to the Pentagon in the days immediately following the attack. In the past, I'd jokingly commented that it was great to be nonessential if it meant a day off. Now, as the aide to the Chairman, there was no question that I had to return to work. Tangibly aware of death all around me, I found it hard to stay focused. Smoke hung heavily in the air, seeping into my clothing and hair. I wished I were anywhere else.

Unable to sit still while my boss attended a meeting at the White House, I aimlessly walked the deadly quiet halls of the Pentagon with leaden feet. Approaching the innermost corridor, I peered through the ceiling-high windows at the surreal scene across the center courtyard. A fireman stood at the top of a long extension ladder, spraying water onto the roof where bright orange flames shot skyward.

It was almost twenty-four hours since the attack, and the Pentagon was still burning. How many fire drills had I participated in during my two-year assignment, knowing there was no danger? We'd evacuated the building and stood outside in the rain or snow to practice. Now, there I stood in a building that was actually on fire, and we were expected to continue working.

The few people in sight walked past me in a daze. I felt like they looked.

Passing the Pentagon's River Entrance on the way back to my office, a line of young soldiers in fatigues paraded soberly in the opposite direction. I recognized them from their impeccable bearing as members of the elite Army Honor Guard, the 3rd US Infantry. These were the soldiers who marched on the parade field at our ceremonies and conducted dignified military funerals at Arlington Ceremony. It was strange to see them in fatigues instead of their spotless dress blues. In response to my inquiry, one young soldier informed me they'd been tasked to search through the rubble for victims of the attack.

It was no wonder their faces were stony.

I returned to my office and sat at my desk, staring at the schedule from the trip we hadn't completed. Suddenly I heard shouts in the hallway. Someone banged on the door and frantically yelled, "Get out! Get out of the building now!"

Heart racing, I opened the door to find a torrent of people rushing toward the nearest exit, many of them running.

"It's another plane!" someone shouted. "Hurry!"

I joined the panicked crowd and hurried to the nearest exit. The guards shooed us along, convinced an attack was imminent. I stepped out into the sunshine and moved to the far end of the parade field. Standing among the edgy group, I searched the sky, dreading what I might see, and praying there would be no more carnage.

"It's a false alarm," a guard announced from the steps. "You can come back in now."

Going back into the building was the last thing I wanted to do. I returned to my office with a sense of vulnerability I'd never before experienced.

It was no easier going to work in the days that followed. I could turn off the television, but there was no escaping the constant reminder that the place we'd thought was invulnerable had been so violently violated. Working in a building where 189 colleagues had been killed was hard to come to grips with. These were people just like me, men and women I had worked with. Some of them I'd known—like the man with the Santa Claus beard who spent his lunch hour passing out candy to unsuspecting strangers, just to see their smiles. If it could happen to people like the Candy Man, it could happen to any of us.

I volunteered to escort some of the victims' family members to a memorial service the following week. My intentions were good, but for me, that turned out to be a painful mistake. I had never been so up-close-and-personal to such raw, aching grief. The duty was almost more than I could bear. I sincerely empathized with the families I escorted, but it hurt too much to imagine what they were going through. At the end of the day I hurried home, relieved that I could escape their anguish, and feeling secretly guilty for having such thoughts. I prayed that I would never know the kind of pain I'd been witness to that day.

Until that point, the only deaths I had experienced were those of my grandparents. Their passing was sad, but expected at their age. I had a happy childhood, raised in a loving, functional family. My parents weren't at all religious, and while I often wondered what I was missing when my friends went off to church, I never felt the need in my younger years to search for the meaning of life. I believed in a higher power, but never gave much thought to my fuzzy concept of God.

September 11th changed all that. In the weeks that followed, I wondered about the victims. Why had so many been in the wrong place at the wrong time? Had each of them fulfilled their life's mission, and was it simply "their time"? What about the people who hadn't gone to work for some reason and were spared? Why were they so lucky and others weren't? And how did the victims' families find the strength to cope with their losses?

These types of questions awoke a long-time curiosity I'd had with near-death experiences, life after death, and with the possibility that we can communicate with those who have crossed over. For years I had frequented New Age bookstores, but my interest in metaphysics wasn't something I discussed with my military colleagues. Stories of those left behind who received loving messages through mediums gave me hope and comfort, but I kept my interests and beliefs mostly to myself.

In spite of these forays into the metaphysical world, on September 11, 2001, my thoughts were still more firmly focused on the material world than the spiritual. I was very good at practicing denial about death. I hadn't yet learned that death has a lot to teach us about life—a lesson I was destined to learn the hard way.

Think back today, but don't despair:
Those long gone, they still are there—
Urging all to trust and pray
That more will see the light some day.

For now, do what small part you can
To carry out your role in God's plan—
Growing always in love and light,
Striving ever to do what's right,

Forgiving others who strike out in pain . . .
This kind of thought is never in vain.
For love's the only thing that's real,
The only way to truly heal.

Release the anger, but never forget
Into your hearts true love to let.
Hate and anger were the cause,
So do not give them further pause.

Only when man can love one another
Living together like sister and brother
Can peace and love then truly reign
And stop the spread of further pain.

A lofty goal—impossible, you say,
But man will never see the day
Until these truths he does enact.
Your future rests in this one fact.

2

Our Susan

September 11th showed me that life is very short and that we should live our dreams while we still can. My husband and I had long shared the dream of selling our house and cars and sailing off into the sunset on our sailboat. I took the lessons of 9/11 to heart and put in my Navy retirement papers. I wasn't eligible to retire until June of 2003, but within 24 hours after my retirement ceremony, we set sail on our 46-foot sloop, *Liberty*, and left Washington in our wake.

For three years we led an idyllic life of travel and adventure on the sea, free from rudeness and road rage, far from the daily barrage of negative news. We'd dreamed of sailing across the Atlantic Ocean, and we did so, achieving a major milestone for myself as a sailor. We then sailed on through the Mediterranean for the next year and a half.

As cruisers, we shunned television, but we kept up with the headlines. Books were our main source of entertainment, but those in English were hard to come by after we crossed the Atlantic. When we sailed to a U.S. Navy base in Sicily, one of our first stops was the base book store, where a tempting title caught my eye: *Talking to Heaven—A Medium's Message of Life After Death*.

I'd read several books about mediums in the past, but I'd never heard of this particular author, James Van Praagh. Little did I know that in our long absence, mediums had gone mainstream. There was now a TV show called *Medium*, and some guy named John Edward was talking to spirits on his own hit show.

I read Van Praagh's stories as we sailed to Greece and on to Montenegro. As with other books of its type, there was no shortage of tales about loved ones comforted by messages from beyond. I wondered, not for the first time, why I felt so drawn to this genre. I felt fortunate that unlike many of the families in *Talking to Heaven*, I'd led a charmed life. I was forty-four years old and had successfully avoided the kind of tragedy I read about in the book or heard about in the news. The memories of 9/11 still weighed heavily on my mind, but I tried not to dwell on them.

My parents were alive and healthy, my father still nimble in his nineties. My sister and brother were married and happy with families of their own. My husband, who I cherished, was fit and strong. While I didn't have children of my own, I shared the love of Ty's daughters, Elisabeth and Susan. Elisabeth was a free spirit, enjoying a life much like our own, with just enough work to feed her lust for travel and adventure. Susan was like her father in a different way: she had dedicated her life in service to her country as a sergeant in the United States Marine Corps.

Life was good as we sailed north in the Adriatic Sea. Everyone we cared about was doing well. In fact, there was a new family member on the way: our first grandchild. We'd flown back to the States for Susan's wedding the previous December. She and her husband, Warren, had wasted no time; it was June now and Susan was six months pregnant.

We were cruising along the coast of Croatia, anchored off a deserted island, when I had a strange dream. It was remarkable in that the images were so clear. Unlike most dreams that slip away like misty memories when you try to recall them, these images stayed with me. In the dream I was at a party with people I didn't know, when my stepdaughter Susan stepped out of the crowd. She walked right up to me and said with a beautiful smile, "We're fine. The baby and I are very happy."

The dream was so strong and clear that I shared it with Ty the next morning as soon as he woke up. We'd emailed Susan in the past couple of weeks, but she, like her sister, was a poor correspondent and rarely responded. I felt the dream was trying to tell me something, and I said to Ty, "We need to email Susan again." He did so that morning, but we knew it would be a while before we got an answer.

Two days later, we received an email from Elisabeth asking us to phone home. There was no urgency in her message. The subject line simply read, "Important." She'd been discussing finances with her father lately, so we figured she needed some advice. There were no phones on the island where we were anchored, so we sailed toward a more populated area the following day. It was late afternoon when we finally arrived at a town with a pay phone.

The number Elisabeth provided was for Warren's cell phone. Liz had been staying with him and Susan for the past week. I stood at Ty's side while he dialed from an open booth in a quiet park. It was a treat to talk to family, so when Warren answered, I leaned in close to listen.

"What's up?" Ty asked cheerfully.

"Nothing good," Warren answered.

Elizabeth's email was so matter-of-fact that we hadn't expected that anything was wrong. Hearing the flat tone of Warren's voice, my mind instantly went on alert. I felt a pang of fear that they'd lost the baby.

That would have been bad enough. The truth was far, far worse.

I couldn't hear what Warren said next, but Ty slumped against the phone booth and cried out, "No, Warren, not Susan!"

My mind raced. It was obvious that something awful had happened. I felt an instant protective urge to shelter Ty from whatever news he'd already heard. Susan was the apple of his eye, his precious baby girl. If anything had happened to her . . . well, it just wasn't thinkable. Whatever it was, she would be okay. Standing at my husband's side, I willed it to be so.

But there was nothing I or anyone else could do.

Ty turned to me and with a look of utter dismay said, "Susan is gone."

The words hung in the air as I tried to make sense of them.

Susan–is–gone.

It was an impossible sentence: a name that was precious to us, followed by an inconsequential verb and an irreversibly final modifier that were never meant to be joined together.

We clutched each other in anguished disbelief as Warren filled in the details. Our beautiful young sergeant had been reporting for duty, crossing the flight line outside her squadron's hangar. She was in a hurry to greet her Marine husband who'd pulled the shift ahead of her. The sky in the distance was dark, but it wasn't yet raining. Suddenly, a jagged streak of lightning reached down from the clouds, striking Susan to the ground in a literal bolt out of the blue. Warren was the first one at her side, but there was nothing he could do for her or the baby.

Ty and I cried out a string of anguished *No*'s in a futile effort to negate the act of nature that had claimed the life of our daughter and her unborn son. Paramedics and hospital personnel had worked on Susan for seven hours, we learned, but she never regained consciousness.

As Ty and I stumbled back to the boat, I suddenly remembered my dream. The image lingered as clear as ever, as did Susan's pronouncement that she and the baby were fine and happy. I analyzed the timeline and shook my head. She had appeared to me the day *before* she was killed. Why not *after*?

Van Praagh's book sprung to mind. He'd written that the soul sometimes knows when its time on the physical plane is over, even if the physical mind isn't aware of its imminent passing. When I read those words, I'd found them hard to swallow. In fact—my apologies to the author—I'd found the concept so outrageous that I'd thrown the book in the trash.

Could the medium Van Praagh have been right after all? Had Susan's soul somehow sensed that she would be leaving the Earth plane the following day? Had she come to me in my dreams to give our family a message?

Such ethereal thoughts were quickly overtaken by the more pressing need to find our way home in time for Susan's funeral. I stood at the helm of our boat as Ty went forward to take in the anchor. I watched in horror as my husband—always my rock in a crisis—fell to his knees in grief, collapsing in a sobbing huddle on the foredeck. I'd known Susan for fourteen years and loved her from the start, as did everyone who met her. Her death was a terrible blow to me, but seeing the man I loved in such soul-searing pain compounded the breathtaking weight that pressed against my chest.

It would take us two days to travel from the tiny island in Croatia where we'd received the news to Susan's base in Havelock, North Carolina. We were on our own, trying to make travel arrangements in a strange language with brains that refused to work. Our only comfort was Rudy, our long-haired miniature dachshund. We couldn't leave him behind in a strange country, so he traveled with us in his Samsonite travel bag on an endless succession of ferries, trains, taxis, and airplanes. While in transport he was supposed to remain in his bag, but every so often we opened the zippered window of his suitcase and his little red head would pop out. Rudy licked our tears and watched us with soulful brown eyes that told us he knew something was terribly wrong.

We arrived in North Carolina and gathered with Warren, Elisabeth, and Susan's mother, all equally distraught. The shock and grief of Susan's sudden death was etched on everyone's face, exactly as it had been on the families of the 9/11 victims I'd accompanied just after the attacks. Then, as an escort officer, I'd scurried away from such palpable pain. Now, there was nothing to do but bear it.

It seemed impossible to imagine that anything could be more painful than hearing the news that every parent dreads, but no shortage of anguishing moments followed that initial shock. The ensuing days were a numbing succession of blows that battered our hearts like a boxer's unpadded fists: the unthinkable sight of Susan's smiling face above her obituary in the local paper . . . the unimaginable sign at the main gate of the Marine Corps base announcing our daughter's memorial service . . . the unbearable experience of holding my husband's shaking shoulders at three o'clock in the morning as he wrote Susan's eulogy—the ultimate farewell for his little girl . . . .

The viewing at the funeral home was meant to give us a sense of finality, a chance to say goodbye. For me, it served an unforeseen purpose that would change the course of my life.

I stood at the flag-draped casket looking down at Susan's body. I recognized the dress uniform, but I felt as if I were looking at a stranger. I had seen lifeless bodies before, but the transformation in Susan was shocking. Even though I was alone, I spoke aloud the thought that assaulted my brain: *That's not Susan . . . That's not Susan . . . .*

The three words ran through my mind like a mantra. Yes, I was in shock, but in that moment of absolute clarity, I knew that everything I'd read in books about the afterlife was true: that the soul survives the change called death. What I was looking at was merely the vessel that had lovingly housed my stepdaughter's spirit for 27 years—a spirit far brighter than the bolt of lightning that had struck all of us to our knees and changed our lives in an instant. Yes, the body before me would return to ashes, but I realized then that Susan's vibrant spirit could never be destroyed.

Susan's funeral the following day was made bearable only by the love we all shared for her and by the dignity and loving care of the Marines with whom she'd served. With Susan's dog tags and helmet hanging from her rifle planted solemnly in her boots before us, I glanced sideways at the open casket at the front of the chapel. I felt no need to approach it again, for I'd already realized that Susan wasn't there.

Sitting in the church pew, I made my first feeble attempts to connect with her spirit mentally until the rude crack of a volley of rifles shocked me back to attention. The gun salute was followed by the lonely wail of Taps played by a solo bugle somewhere in the distance. I tried to believe the honor was meant for someone else, but when Susan's commanding officer handed a folded flag to her mother and father, I could no longer deny reality.

We filed out of the chapel, leading a somber parade of family, friends, and stoic Marines. It had been raining when the ceremony started, but we emerged beneath a brilliant blue sky. Ahead of us a hearse stood silently waiting, but around us the trees were far from still. All heads turned skyward in surprise as the wind rushed back and forth, causing a troupe of dancing leaves to swirl around us in gusts that can only be described as playful.

Ty squeezed my hand and I looked over to find his eyes filled with wonder. "That's Susan," he said, standing with head cocked as he watched the strangely frolicking branches.

"I feel her," he said, and his lips curled upward in the first smile that had crossed his face in days.

I eyed him curiously. A retired destroyer captain, Ty had always been firmly rooted in the material world. I could clearly see that he wasn't just saying the words. He meant them. I'd been hesitant to share my interest in life after death with him, but in that magical moment I sensed that a door had been opened, if only a crack.

My mission was now clear: If there was a way of contacting Susan's spirit, I was going to find it.

Lie down here beside me.
Rest your weary head.
Do not cry not in mourning,
For I'm not really dead.

I always step beside you
When my name you call.
I'm here to dry your tears.
I will not let you fall.

I dance in every raindrop.
I ride upon the wind.
I whisper softly in your mind,
For I am there within.

Do not cry not in mourning.
My spirit lives forever.
It's only in your mind
That you think you'll see me never.

Just call my name and I am there.
I step right to your side.
And when you want to feel me close
Your wish I do abide.

It's subtle, this my energy.
Quite difficult to hear.
But when you feel a shiver slight
Just know that I am near.

3

Coincidence

Books written in English are hard to come by in Croatia. I knew that the choice of topics would be slim once we left the U.S. and returned to our boat. My overriding interest was to find out all I could about life after death, so we stopped at a bookstore on the way to the airport. The New Age section had no shortage of titles that looked interesting, but I could only carry so many books in my luggage.

I scanned five shelves of potential purchases. Ty stood nearby checking his watch. I knew this was my one shot to find out how to contact Susan's spirit. Past experience with asking for higher guidance had proven unfailingly reliable, so I focused my intention on the best possible outcome and silently asked, "Which of these books am I supposed to read?"

I ran my hand in front of the shelves like a metal detector. Three times it stopped. Each time I stuck out my index finger and plucked a book that seemed to call out to me, *This one . . . and this one . . . and this one.*

I paid for my purchases and we headed for the airport. I began reading the first book on the flight across the Atlantic. *Walking in the Garden of Souls* proved to be an excellent choice. The author, George Anderson, was obviously a gifted medium. The comforting messages he related from years of contacting the spirit world gave me hope that Ty and I would one day receive such a message from our Susan.

Our flight landed in Venice, where we decided to stay
for a couple of days and decompress before the remaining
journey by train, ferry, and bus. Any other time I would
have been thrilled to explore the city's famed canals, but with
Susan's funeral still fresh in our minds, we wandered through
the narrow streets and piazzas as if drugged.

We retreated to our room at midday, and I took my book
to the balcony. Ty joined me with a sailing magazine and we
sat side by side reading in the peace of the secluded hotel. A
short while later, the sound of nearby voices made me raise
my head and look around. I could see no one on the adjoining balconies. The voices seemed unusually close, so I set my
book down, walked into our room, and stared, confused, at
the source of the sound: The television set, which had been
turned off when we went to the balcony, was now on.

I picked up the remote control and turned it over several
times in my hands. I pointed it at the TV and hit the power
switch three times, turning it off, then very deliberately turning it on, then off again. It worked just as it was supposed to,
but it took deliberate effort. I returned to the balcony and
said to Ty, "The TV turned itself on."

He glanced up and made a little "hunh" sound, then went
back to reading.

I sat down and returned to my book as well. The very next
paragraph I read made me stop and go back to re-read the words.
With flawless timing, George Anderson confirmed that those in
the spirit world often let their loved ones know they're around by
manipulating lights, electrical appliances, and electronic equip-
ment.

"My God, Ty, listen to this," I said, and read him the quote.
He looked a bit nonplussed.

"When's the last time you saw a TV turn itself on?" I asked.
"Never."

"Me neither."

I knew I was in a vulnerable position—wanting badly to receive a sign from Susan that she was around us in spirit. I sat back and closed my eyes. Was this just a coincidence? If it was, it was a big one. I allowed myself the faintest of hope that the unusual event was more than simple serendipity, and that I'd been led to the book for this important lesson.

The rest of our journey had its difficulties. The train from Italy through Slovenia was delayed by a workers' strike. We barely made the last ferry to Croatia, and when we arrived at the northern end of the island where we'd left our boat, there was no public transportation for the remaining forty kilometers. We spoke no Croatian, but using hand gestures and pointing to a map, we cajoled a tow truck driver to give us a ride.

The man didn't look particularly pleased at the intrusion, but he seemed resigned to helping us. He tossed our luggage onto the open bed where he would normally strap a car, and the three of us climbed into the cab. Squeezed between the two men, I clutched our small Samsonite bag in my lap. The driver motioned for me to put it in the back with the others, and I shook my head. I reached down, pulled back the zipper, and out popped a furry red head.

The driver pulled back in surprise, then his eyes lit up and his mouth broke into a wide grin. Our little icebreaker, Rudy, had done it again. We learned the word for "dog" in Croatian and the driver learned it in English. Then we found out that both he and I spoke enough Italian to communicate without our hands. We arrived at the southern end of the island, and he went out of his way to drop us off right at the pier where we'd left our boat.

Our long trip was over. We were back at our floating home, but the painful memories from the day we'd left still lingered in the air. We'd previously planned to sail farther north along the coast, but Ty and I had lost all desire to stay a day longer in Croatia than we had to.

The next morning we got under way and headed south. By then, I had finished *Walking in the Garden of Souls* and began the second book to which I'd been led, another by George Anderson entitled *Lessons From the Light*. I'd read books by mediums in the past, but always out of mere curiosity. Now I read with growing excitement the seemingly irrefutable evidence that life doesn't end with the death of the physical body. I became convinced that I needed to find a medium as good as George Anderson for Ty and myself.

Two days into our southerly passage, I'd finished most of book number two. I sat in the cockpit reading the final pages as Ty manned the helm.

"Hey, Suzanne," he said.

I looked up.

"Have you noticed the yellow butterfly that's been following us for the past two days?"

I looked aft and spotted it. In fact, I had noticed it, but lost in my thoughts, I hadn't paid attention. Now I realized how unusual it was to see a butterfly so far out on the water. I glanced at the shoreline, a thin blue line in the distance. The nearest land was a good four miles away.

"I wonder what it's doing way out here," I said.

"Kind of strange," Ty said.

I went back to my book, and there, on the very page I'd been reading when Ty interrupted me, was a message straight from heaven.

"My God," I said for the second time in a week, "listen to this . . . ." I read aloud George Anderson's timely claim that "signs from the Infinite Light can often be right under our noses . . . as subtle as a tiny butterfly in December."

Ty blinked in surprise, looked aft, and said, "Or on the Adriatic Sea?"

I went on to read aloud Anderson's story of a woman who began seeing ubiquitous yellow butterflies shortly after the death of her son. At that moment, the butterfly that had fluttered back and forth in our wake for two days drew even with the cockpit where we sat, then flew directly between Ty and me before heading for shore.

Was it yet another coincidence? A fluke of nature? If so, then so was the swarm of yellow butterflies that hovered overhead as we arrived at the island of Mljet later that day. Six other boats lined the sea wall beside us, yet ours was the only one with the yellow winged visitors who made their presence known for half an hour on that very special evening.

The next day, rather than get under way right away, Ty and I set out on a hike. A winding path led through thick woods to the island's highest point. Still dazed and numb, we walked in silence. Instead of staring at my feet, I stared pointedly at the trail ahead. By then I'd read dozens of accounts in my two books describing wispy figures that appeared to those who were grieving. As we trudged upward, I willed Susan to make her presence known to me.

Higher and higher we climbed, and with each step I grew more despondent. Why couldn't I sense her? Surely all the miraculous stories I'd read pointed to some kind of existence after death.

We reached the summit and turned to retrace our steps. Ty walked on ahead of me now, a good fifty yards down the trail.

Discouraged, but not defeated, I continued my efforts.

Susan, I prayed, *please give me some kind of sign that you're around. We so desperately need to know that you're not gone forever.*

Knowing what I know now about the spirit world, I can just picture Susan at that moment. I'm sure she was shaking her head at me, laughing, and saying, *Haven't you noticed all the butterflies I've been sending you?*

Susan was laughing because just then, a flicker of movement from the left caught my attention. I turned my head and saw a yellow butterfly with a red dot on its back flying straight at me. It arrived at my side, flew a complete circle around me, then bounced straight into my chest at the level of my heart. I stopped in my tracks and watched, stunned, as the butterfly then flew in a direct line down the trail toward Ty.

Incredulous, I called out his name. The shock in my voice caused him to stop and turn. The butterfly had reached him by then, and I watched as it flew a complete circle around him, as well, before bouncing into what would have been his chest had I not caused him to turn so suddenly. As it was, the butterfly touched him right at the level of his heart, before flying off into the woods.

I stood rooted in place, awestruck, and reviewed the unusual events of the past week: the self-starting television set, the butterfly that accompanied us for two days at sea, the special swarm around our boat, and now a butterfly that flew a specific and meaningful path, as if being guided.

I may be a bit slow at times, but I finally got it. I wasn't able to sense Susan's spirit directly, but somehow—perhaps with the assistance of more experienced helpers on the other side—she'd been sending us signs in direct answer to my prayers.

I continued down the trail, my steps a bit lighter. There was no doubt in my mind that something spiritual was going on and that Susan was behind it. God was my witness, and—thank goodness—so was my husband. The skeptic in me could not deny what had been happening.

My next step was to find a good medium.

We can move mountains if we wish,
But there's no real point in this.
A tiny insect we can ask
To do our task.

It's all one Spirit
But you cannot hear it
As we whisper to the butterfly
To do our bidding, and it does comply.

We can move them with our thought.
Free will, have they not.
All cooperating as a whole,
For it is all just one great soul.

4

Evidence

They say that when the student is ready, the teacher will appear. That teacher appeared for me in the form of B. Anne Gehman. I'd never heard of Anne Gehman until I read her name in the third and final book I was guided to buy in my quest to learn about the afterlife. Aptly named, *The Afterlife Experiments* proved to be the most convincing of the three books that communication with the spirit world was possible.

The author, Dr. Gary Schwartz, a scientist and psychologist with a Ph.D from Harvard, gathered a handful of credible mediums to prove or disprove the existence of an afterlife. He conducted strictly controlled experiments with these mediums over a period of several years. The result was a set of highly persuasive data supporting the hypothesis that consciousness survives the death of the brain.

My criteria for finding a medium to reunite us with Susan was almost as stringent as Dr. Schwartz's. I wasn't about to consult the Yellow Pages for some dial-a-psychic, nor do a random search online for an unknown medium. Whoever I chose had to get past the skeptical minds of two career naval officers. So far, Ty had tolerantly gone along with my talk of consulting a medium. If the one I chose turned out to be no good, I might lose his support to try a second time.

The mediums in Schwartz's book proved themselves repeatedly in blind experiments. They provided evidence of communication with the other side with percentages of accuracy that far exceeded random chance. I felt that if I could get a reading with one of the credible mediums featured in *The Afterlife Experiments,* I would be able to trust the information I was given.

By the time I finished the book, we had sailed to Greece. Sitting at an Internet café, I Googled each of the names from Schwartz's experiments. Four had fancy websites and long waiting lists. The one medium in the group who intrigued me the most—Anne Gehman—didn't have her own website.

Further searching revealed that Anne had used her gifts to help members of the FBI, Congress, various police departments around the country, and top governmental officials. According to news articles, Anne Gehman was not only a medium, but also the pastor of her own Spiritualist church. I'd never heard of Spiritualism (with a capital S).

I changed search parameters and discovered that Spiritualism was not only a religion, but a science and a philosophy, as well. Its followers dated back to the 19th century. The Spiritualists' beliefs and principles seemed reasonable and non-threatening, and seemed to allow room for a broad spectrum of religious beliefs.

As I read the Spiritualists' nine Declaration of Principles, I realized that my personal beliefs fit perfectly with theirs. Why else would I be seeking a medium if I didn't believe that life is eternal, that the spirit continues after the transition we call death, and that it's possible to communicate with those who've crossed to the other side?

I found a website that featured Anne Gehman's Center for Spiritual Enlightenment. I scrolled down and stopped, stunned, when I read the church's address. The most impressive medium from *The Afterlife Experiments* had a church less than twenty minutes from a rental home that Ty and I maintained in northern Virginia. In light of Susan's death, he and I had decided just days earlier to leave the boat in Turkey and reoccupy that house in order to be closer to family for a while. I couldn't help but marvel at yet another seeming coincidence from the third and final book I'd been guided to buy.

Upon our arrival in northern Virginia, I wasted no time in trying to set up a reading with Anne. To my disappointment, I learned that she'd recently had hip replacement surgery and wouldn't be giving readings for a few months. She was, however, teaching a once-weekly class at her church on the philosophy of Spiritualism. I signed up for the class and resigned myself to wait however long it took to get a reading with her.

For six consecutive Tuesday evenings I sat in the front row of Anne's class, enthralled by her stories. Here was a woman who could actually see spirits objectively—with her own eyes, not just in her mind's eye. She was a born medium, and told of giving readings to her teddy bears in the woodshed behind her house at age five, long before she or her family knew what mediumship was.

The class included instruction in meditation, a practice Anne said was critical to developing mediumship. I had learned this from my earlier research and had begun daily meditation shortly after Susan's death as a way to sense her spirit. Until Anne's class, I hadn't felt much benefit from the practice. More often than not I'd fall asleep and wonder if I was wasting my time.

Little did I know that bit by bit, the time I spent sitting in the silence had been training my brain to be still. I didn't know until I attended Anne's class that the spirit world is a realm of pure energy. Vibrations from the spirit dimension are so fine, so subtle, that unless one learns to quiet the mind, it's nearly impossible to detect them. With Anne's encouragement, I decided to continue my efforts.

One evening in class Anne explained that ordinary objects become imprinted with the energy of anyone who comes in contact with them. She asked us to pair up and exchange a piece of jewelry with the person seated next to us. Our assignment was to hold the person's belonging and see if we could sense anything about the owner, a practice called psychometry.

My partner handed me her bracelet and I squeezed it in my palm. Instantly, the word "headache" popped into my mind. Surprised, but curious, I asked my partner if she had a headache.

"As a matter of fact," she said, "I do."

I did a small double-take and looked at the bracelet.

"Try to get at least three things about the person," Anne said to the class.

I squeezed the bracelet again and heard the words "new car"—words that seemed to come out of thin air and had nothing to do with me. "Do you have a new car?" I asked, intrigued by my earlier success.

Anne walked by at just that moment and gently admonished me, "Don't ask questions. Tell her what you sense."

"Okay," I said, feeling somewhat foolish. "You have a new car."

"As a matter of fact," the woman said, smiling, "I do."

"Really?" I was amazed. How was it that I was hearing these words? Was it possible that my months of meditation had something to do with this new sense of hearing?

"One more," my partner encouraged me.

"Okay." I waited a moment, sitting quietly, just as I did in meditation, then, "Son . . . Son . . . " I said, "I'm just hearing the word 'son.'"

The woman glanced at her lap, then back at me. "I have a son on the other side."

"Oh, my God."

How to explain it? I hadn't gone to the class expecting any more than to be in Anne Gehman's presence and learn about mediumship. I hadn't expected to have any kind of personal experience, yet each of the three things I'd told the woman held meaning for her.

The concept of psychometry had sounded a bit crazy to me. How could I tell something about another person just by holding their jewelry? Yet, I couldn't deny that I had heard the words—subtle as they might be—as if they were my own thoughts.

I handed the woman one of my rings, but she failed to tell me anything about my life that I could confirm. I felt a bit embarrassed for her as we went around the room and reported on what we'd sensed. My ears perked up instantly, however, when Penny, the woman on my other side, shared her experience with the group.

"When I held my partner's watch," she said, "I became aware of her aunt standing at her side. I heard the name 'Hazel,' and was able to describe how Hazel died."

The other woman confirmed that her mother's sister had died exactly as Penny said, and that her name had been Hazel. I listened, astonished. For the rest of the session, all I could think about was talking with Penny. As soon as class let out, I approached her.

"Excuse me," I said, for until that evening, we hadn't spoken. "Are you a medium?" I asked.

"Well, yes, I suppose I am," she said, somewhat hesitantly.

"Do you give readings?"

"On occasion," she replied.

I took a deep breath. Anne wasn't giving readings, but that wasn't a showstopper. Here was the answer to my prayers. All I wanted was someone who I trusted that could sense spirits. Penny had demonstrated this ability quite well. Best of all, neither she, nor anyone else in the class, including Anne, knew my last name or knew about my loss. I didn't want to ever wonder if the medium I chose had found the tribute to Susan I'd posted on our sailing website. The skeptic in me needed to find a medium who knew nothing about Susan or about me. It appeared that I'd found that medium.

When Penny agreed to give readings to both me and to Ty, my mind raced. What if Penny gave me only non-evidential messages that anyone could make up? Would I simply have to go on faith alone? What if Susan didn't come through? Would we then have to face the fact that she was gone forever? I knew in my heart that I wouldn't be satisfied unless Penny identified Susan and gave details about her that she couldn't possibly know.

Four days later, Ty and I showed up at Penny's 7th floor condo in an exclusive high rise not far from Washington's National Cathedral. I'd spent the whole drive drumming my fingers on my thighs, well aware of how much hope I was placing on one woman's abilities. The fact that Ty had agreed to accompany me on this admittedly unusual venture spoke of his desire to find answers as well. He said little as we approached Penny's door. I kept up a continuous silent prayer to Susan to not let us down.

Penny informed us that she normally read for only one person at a time, and we agreed that I would sit with her first. She poured Ty a cup of tea, then got him settled into her well-appointed dining room. She and I retreated to a small sitting room overlooking the tree-lined street below. I sat nervously on a brocaded love seat as Penny settled into a high-backed armchair to my left.

She began by asking my full name and birth date. I didn't mind giving this information now, for it would reveal nothing about Susan.

Penny jotted these on a notepad in her lap, then said, "And now, if I could have something of yours to hold that is imbued with your energy, something you wear a lot."

I found it interesting that she would repeat the same exercise we'd done in class, and felt a shiver of excitement. The process had resulted in good things for her the last time we were together. That night I had given my partner the pearl ring from my right hand. Tonight, with everything resting on the results, I went for broke and gave Penny my diamond engagement ring.

The moment Penny touched the ring, her eyes widened and she reared back in her seat.

"Oh!" she said, "What a happy marriage you have! Mmmm! Oh, my goodness me. Well, first of all, I just see all these little children angels, and they're circling around and around with garlands of flowers. You are a very spiritual person, I gather."

I laughed and said, "I'm working on it."

Penny paused, then gave me a beautiful smile. "Happiness is all around you. It's so rare to have someone come to me who is so organically happy."

I sighed, frustrated. Yes, until Susan's death I'd been quite happy.

"Why do you need a reading? You have everything," Penny said.

And I thought, "No, not anymore."

"So, you are just completely blessed," she said.

I was beginning to get restless. While it was nice to hear such positive words, it wasn't at all why I'd come. "There's a spirit I was hoping would show up," I said, hesitant to give even the slightest bit of information. "That's why I wanted the reading."

"Oh, you wanted a reading for a particular spirit?"

Why else? I thought, but said instead, "Any that would show up, but one in particular."

Penny sat back and looked around the room. Meanwhile, I prayed that those little cherubs supposedly circling around me would go and find Susan.

Without notice, Penny squinted and asked, "Do you have a headache? I have a tremendous headache suddenly."

"No," I answered, and felt a chill. I knew from my research that mediums will often sense how a person died from a physical sensation within their own body. The lightning had struck Susan in the head.

Penny wasn't letting it go. "Do you have a headache or allergies? I'm tingly all over, like little electrical impulses."

I was finding it hard to sit still now, but I answered no again.

"Okay," she said. "That might be me instead of you. But it was so sudden, this thing." She touched her forehead. "It's like . . . actually, I think it *does* relate to you because I don't—I can't express it exactly, but it's like the headache of Zeus and Athena."

My memory of mythology was a bit weak, but I knew who Zeus was: *the God of lightning bolts*!

I pictured the mighty figure standing atop a mountain holding in his hand a jagged bolt of lightning just like the one that had struck Susan, and the tears began.

Penny didn't seem to notice how deeply her words had shaken me. She shifted gears and went back to giving me information unrelated to Susan.

"I'm asking what your work is," she said, "and this is really unusual in the sense that I think you're reaching into the highest angelic realm. The work that you should be doing relates to some kind of service . . . ."

"I've been meditating and praying to be led to what I should do," I admitted.

"Take a moment and shut your eyes and breathe, because they're right here now," she said, "two very powerful angels standing right behind you. And if, before you begin your work, you ask them to be working through you, it will always happen."

"I do that," I said. "Before I write."

"That's perfect," Penny said, then she paused.

I held my breath. Enough about me. I wanted to get back to the lightning bolts.

"Well, there's someone here who wants to speak to you, but I'm not getting very . . . much . . . except a little tug, like this . . . ." She tugged at her sleeve. "And it's a woman—well, really, it's more like a young girl, a young girl in her twenties. She was a relative . . . and died unexpectedly. Do you have someone who died young and unexpectedly?"

My throat instantly constricted. "Oh, yes," I said as my heart pounded. "That's why I'm here."

"You don't have to explain," Penny said, "because I'm trying to listen to what she's saying, and it's better if you don't talk to me. I'll tell you what I'm getting, even if it's a mistake."

What she'd said so far was no mistake. If Penny had wanted to give a flawless reading, she only had to tell me that she sensed a great-grandmother with gray hair who died when her heart gave out. Anyone could fake that kind of detail. What she'd given me was exactly what I'd been praying to hear, with accuracy no one could fake: the headache, the electrical impulses, the lightning bolt reference, and now the presence of a young woman in her twenties, who had died suddenly.

What Penny said next turned my tears into sobs.

"And now there's a second person who is a younger child. She's holding this child by the hand. It's somebody from the other side that she's taking care of and she wants to present this child to you. Um, they're fine!" Penny said, giving me the same message Susan had given me in my vivid dream. "They're wonderful, and she loves you . . . enormously. And, um, and 'don't be unhappy,' or 'don't cry, don't cry . . . .'"

Not crying was impossible. "Just tell her to come back for her dad," I begged.

"What?"

"Tell her to stay here for her dad."

"Stay here for her dad," Penny repeated. "Okay. You can tell her that. I just got chills. If you want, you can talk to her now and I'll hold her, hold the energy field like a radio for you and you talk to her with your heart. And if you can't hear her, I'll tell you what she's saying. 'Mother' is the word I get. And I'm just having waves of heat and energy at the heart. Enormous waves of love. And this child that she has presented is still there, but hanging back a little shyly, as if he, uh, doesn't know to come crawl on your lap."

I had to remind myself to breathe, for breathing was the only way I knew I wasn't dreaming. This evidence from Susan expressed through this living angel, Penny, was beyond my dreams.

"I've just gotten a word I don't understand at all, which is the word 'Ruby,'" Penny said.

"Rudy?" I asked. Susan had loved our little dachshund, as she loved all animals.

"Could be Rudy. A lot of it I only hear little pieces of. Anyway, she just sat herself down here next to you." Penny laughed happily.

"Do you sense that?" I asked, incredulous, "Or do you see it?"

"Well, I sort of see it."

"Is she around a lot?"

"Are you around a lot?" she asked the space beside me.

I glanced to my side and bit my lip.

"No. No, she's not," Penny said. "She has a lot of stuff to do, but she looks in now and again . . . at night, particularly . . . at night when you're sleeping, because that's a time when it's possible to come through, in a dream or in that hypnogogic state. So she tries sometimes then, but, there's a lot going on on the other side. She has a lot of stuff she's doing and is very happy."

This was exactly what I'd read about in Van Praagh's book. The crazy notion of a spirit world where spirits actually *worked* had landed that book in the trash. Now, I listened eagerly for more.

"'*Mother, mother*'," Penny said. "She doesn't want to leave your side, and so I wonder if it would be possible for your husband to come in."

"Absolutely!" I said, jumping up from the sofa. I hurried to the dining room on shaking legs. Ty looked up when I appeared in the doorway and announced in rapid fire, "You have to come now because there's a young girl in her twenties who died unexpectedly and she has a baby with her and she wants to talk to you."

He took in my words and my tear-stained face, and his lips became a thin line. He followed me wordlessly to the other room and took a seat in the empty chair across from Penny. She asked for his full name and birth date and I squirmed anxiously as she wrote his reply.

"I've not tried to read for two people at once," she said, "but we have a spirit here, and it's a young woman, and this repetition of 'mother.'"

Just then, a loud crash caused the three of us to jump. A fern that had been sitting squarely in a large clay pot on a table across the room lay shattered on the floor. Penny frowned at the dirt spread across the linoleum. Ty and I stared at the window, which was only open a few inches. The branches on the trees outside barely moved, certainly not enough to dislodge a heavy planter.

"I'm sorry about that," Penny said, as if it were a normal occurrence to have objects fall to the floor by themselves. "It just jerked me out of this for a moment." She then proceeded to describe Susan correctly as a very nice-looking girl with brown hair and a brown uniform, just as our young Marine once wore.

"And this is your daughter, isn't it, because she's now she's saying 'Daddy'…"

"Yes." It was Ty's turn to choke up.

"Yes. And I don't know if you can feel her embracing you now, but again I'll tell you that if you want to talk to her, I'll hold this energy field, and you say whatever you want to say to her, and she is actually at this moment almost in tears. This means a lot to her to come to you."

The moment seemed surreal as my destroyer captain husband spoke with great emotion to his deceased daughter. He told Susan how much he missed her and loved her, and how much more he would have said to her if he'd had the chance.

"She wants you to know she's very happy," Penny said.

Anyone could have made up those feel-good words, but Penny's description that followed let us know that the sentiments had come from Susan herself.

"She just wants to sit on your lap and wrap her arms around your neck," Penny said, describing exactly the way Susan used to embrace her dad, even at age 27, for—Marine sergeant or not—she was still Daddy's girl.

"She just wants to say, 'I love you.' That's basically the message. Just 'I love you. I love you.'"

Penny suggested that I might be able to sense Susan's presence in the future. For Ty, if he were to write Susan a letter, Penny said, Susan could read it over his shoulder.

"Tell her I'll write to her tonight," Ty said, and I knew then that he believed.

"Okay, I will." Penny paused, then nodded her head. "Now she says it's time for her to go, and she's standing in front of you," she said, looking at Ty, "with her head on your shoulder, her arms around your neck."

I pictured the scene in my mind, but there was no need to use my imagination. I'd seen Susan stand just that way many times when she and her father had to say goodbye.

"Susan …" Ty uttered.

"And again," Penny said, "'I love you, I love you.'"

"I love you too," Ty said softly.

My heart was breaking. The pain was made tolerable, however, by a new sense of comfort that hadn't been there when we arrived.

Penny now cocked her head and smiled at Ty. "The child, meanwhile, has been doing almost nothing except looking at you, sucking his thumb, as it were—but very shy and looking to your daughter for directions."

It was almost too much to bear. The ultrasounds had shown it would be a boy. They had decided to name him Liam Tyler.

Penny paused, then gave a final message to Ty from Susan, "She says, 'I'll wait for your letter tonight.'"

"You can count on it," Ty said, and the set of his jaw told me that he would write that letter.

Thanks to a very gifted medium, I knew as well that our Susan would be looking over his shoulder as he wrote.

When two hearts are joined as one
They always will be linked.
The bonds that do connect you
Can never be extinct.

For love's a potent energy.
Its resonance is great.
And when you share that power,
The greatest link do you create.

Death cannot divide you.
No distance is too far.
No matter if you're here or there,
Joined by love's bond you are.

So grieve not for your loved ones
Who you think have left your side.
Their energy surrounds you –
In your heart it does reside.

To feel it concentrate your thoughts
On how you truly feel.
Recreate the love you shared
And make their presence real.

They're there just waiting for you –
A simple loving thought away.
So hold them firmly in your heart
Until you meet again one day.

5

On a Mission

I had a newfound sense of peace in the days and
weeks following my reading with Penny. I no longer
experienced the hunger and longing to know that Susan's
spirit survived. The hunger was replaced with thirst,
however—thirst for more knowledge about Spiritualism and how I could develop my own spiritual gifts. My
personal library grew considerably with books not just on
Spiritualism, but also on consciousness, physics, religion,
and philosophy.

At first I couldn't understand why more people didn't
know about Spiritualism. I felt the message that this life is
not all there is was far too important to be relegated to a few
esoteric books in the New Age section of a bookstore. My research uncovered a long line of credible mediums dating back
to the mid-1800s, but unfortunately, these were interspersed
with just enough charlatans over the years to make mediumship suspect in mainstream society.

The evidence that Penny brought through proved to
me that as a medium, she was the real deal—as was Anne
Gehman. It seemed unfair that the comforting message of
mediumship should be tainted by a few unscrupulous frauds.
Now that I had found proof that Susan was around, I felt the
stirrings of a new goal. Already a published author, I decided
to write a book that would give Spiritualism more legitimacy
and greater exposure.

I contacted Anne Gehman and asked if we could get together to discuss my ideas. To my delight, she agreed, and invited me to meet her at a local café for lunch. To me, this was like being invited to dine with a celebrity. Over the years, Anne had run in some pretty high circles among the Who's Who of the metaphysical world. Ever humble, Anne didn't seem to notice how nervous I felt as I took a seat across from her in the back booth of the restaurant.

We both ordered a salad and chatted for a while about my experiences in her class. I then told Anne about my reading with Penny and laid out my plan for a book. I felt my ideas were good, but I noticed with a bit of puzzlement that Anne didn't seem to be interested in what I had to say. Her eyes had taken on a dreamy look and she gazed off to the side instead of looking at me as I spoke.

At first I was a bit put off by her seeming inattentiveness, then I recalled Anne telling our class that someone was going to write her biography within the next year. Several class-mates had immediately raised their hands and volunteered to write the book for her. And why not? This was a woman who had given readings to the Speaker of the House, doused for oil for the CEO of a leading petroleum company, and helped solve multiple murders and missing persons cases. I allowed myself the briefest moment to fantasize about such a dream project, then chided myself. Why would Anne Gehman choose me to write her life story?

But now, with Anne's previous comment about a biography fresh in my mind, my pulse quickened. I'd seen her eyes glaze over just like this when a student in the class asked her to predict an event in their future.

I couldn't suppress an exciting thought: *She's checking me out to author her book!*

I experienced an unfamiliar sense of knowing what she was thinking, yet I didn't trust it. Could Anne actually be considering me to write her story? If so, I would certainly be able to get the message of mediumship across, but in a far more entertaining manner than originally planned.

I waited for Anne to raise the issue of her biography, but she remained maddeningly silent. Finally, I came right out and offered to write her story. She gazed off to the left for a moment, then looked me straight in the eye, nodded, and said, "It feels right."

I knew at that moment what it felt like to win the lottery. By the time we left the restaurant, we'd sealed the deal with a handshake.

Three weeks later I sat at the kitchen table in Anne's summer home at the Spiritualist community of Lily Dale, New York. I'd flown in the night before for our initial round of interviews. Anne's husband, Wayne, set a plate of perfectly poached eggs on the table before me. I knew then that I'd be well fed for the week I'd be staying with them in their pink and white cottage.

I took a few bites of breakfast, then got right down to business. Anne had over 70 years of life experiences to share, and we had a lot of ground to cover.

"Okay, Anne," I said, "We need to make your book stand apart from any others out there about psychic-mediums. In other words, we need a 'hook.'" I tapped my finger on the table and said, "So, tell me, what makes you different?"

Anne's eyes narrowed as she pondered my question, then she giggled self-consciously and shrugged her shoulders.

This was not an auspicious start. I put my hands out like a movie director and said, "Help me out here, Anne. I know what makes your life interesting, but I want you to put it into words for me. Why would people want to read your story in particular?"

She bit her lip and said, "Let me think . . . ."

I turned and looked beseechingly at Wayne. While friendly and overtly polite, I'd sensed a hint of resistance from him since my arrival. Anne had hinted earlier that Wayne, a professor of literature at Georgetown University for over 30 years, with a Ph.D in English from Harvard, had at one time expressed an interest in writing his wife's story himself. I could understand why he might not be happy with my presence, but that was between him and Anne. I'd gone there at Anne's request, and had a job to do.

Wayne cleared his throat. "There's so much about Anne's life that's fascinating, but what specifically attracted me to her is her deep spirituality."

Anne reached across the table and patted his hand. I looked at the two of them smiling at each other like newlyweds, and just like that, it hit me.

"Wayne!" I said pointing at him, "*You're* the hook!"

I leaned back in my chair and looked back and forth from husband to wife. Neither of them seemed to follow my thinking.

"Don't you see?" I asked, growing ever more excited. "Anne, it's pretty unusual for a medium to be married to a professor at one of the most prestigious universities in the country, but your story is even more unique because you're married to a former Jesuit priest!"

"Oh, I see what you mean," she said, as Wayne made a humming noise.

My mind kicked into high gear. I'd Googled Wayne's name before going to Lily Dale and had been impressed with his background. An article described his being selected by the students at Georgetown as Professor of the Year along with Wayne's single-minded focus in achieving his dreams.

"Your life is fascinating in its own right," I said. "I could tell both of your stories in alternating chapters, culminating in your unusual marriage."

I could see the book in my mind as if it were already written. The underlying theme would be how two people with divergent beliefs had come together, united by their love for God and for each other.

"People who might never read about a medium would be drawn to a book like this because of your Catholic background. That would make it feel 'safe' for them to explore the topic of mediumship."

Wayne appeared to be giving the idea serious consideration.

"Don't you see," I said, raising my eyebrows, "it would have *mass* appeal!"

They groaned at my pun, but both agreed that the idea had merit. By the end of breakfast *The Priest and the Medium* was born.

The week at Lily Dale passed quickly. I alternated between interviewing Anne and Wayne, filling twice as many cassettes as I'd planned on using. I asked my questions in dedicated sessions on their porch overlooking Cassadaga Lake, as well as during meals and on rides around the local area. One evening we went outside of Lily Dale to a restaurant on Lake Chattaqua. Anne invited her neighbor, Janet Nohavec, to join us.

Ever in journalistic mode, I questioned Janet about her background. Her story was as intriguing as Anne's. Janet had spent four years as a Catholic nun and was now a practicing medium and the pastor of her own Spiritualist church in northern New Jersey. She made a point of telling me that she was British trained. When I asked her what the difference was between British methods and American, she raised her chin.

"It's all about the evidence," she said. "You gotta watch out for mediums who only give you airy-fairy messages. There's no proof in that."

Intrigued, I asked Janet if I might be able to get a reading with her. She told me her waiting list was over a year long. I nodded, impressed that so many people wanted to sit with her, and asked to be placed on the list. I didn't mind waiting for a second chance to be reunited with Susan now that I'd received confirmation that her spirit was around.

Happily, I received further confirmation of Susan's presence much sooner than I'd expected later that week when Anne offered to give me a reading. Anne might not have been British trained like Janet, but as a born medium who had practiced her gifts since childhood, Anne hadn't needed formal training. During our session, she gave me more than enough evidence to prove to me that I had chosen a valid mission in agreeing to write her biography.

Before the reading began, Anne stated for the record that she knew about Susan's death. We had discussed it during our initial conversation when I explained why I felt so driven to write a book about mediumship. She also knew that Susan had been pregnant, but that was the extent of what I'd told her.

"Yes, yes, Susan is here," she said as the reading began. "And I see her holding the baby in her arms." She paused for a moment, then asked, "Was this determined to be a boy? Because it feels like a boy baby to me. And I think she had a couple of names picked out, and I see her using the name of Ty . . . or Tyler."

Liam's middle name, I thought.

Anne's eyes took on that now-familiar dreamy look. "And she seems to want to talk about her transition to the other world. It's almost as if she had some premonition of this. She knew this was going to happen, but she didn't know how or where or what, but subconsciously I think she was well prepared for this somehow."

This wasn't evidence in the true sense of the word, but I couldn't help but think of the dream in which Susan had appeared to me just before her death.

"What she's showing me is that she was immediately taken into the arms of loved ones of the other world," Anne said. "There's a Ber ... Ber ... Bertha? And Bertha was there to take Susan into the other world."

Oh, God, I thought. Ty would not be able to ignore this. His Aunt Bertha had been like a second mother to him when he was a young boy. Anne's words gave me hope that it was true what I'd read: that we are met by loved ones when we cross over. Even more comforting was the thought that we would see our loved ones again when it was our turn to pass to the other side.

Anne laughed now. "She has a nice sense of humor, doesn't she? It's as if she's trying to be sort of playful. And she tells me to tell you that you will be growing together as you unfold spiritually and mediumistically."

This caught me by surprise. I would be growing mediumistically? It wasn't something I had considered, but I found the idea exciting.

I asked Anne if Susan could tell me anything about her biological mother, Angie. Anne squinted. "Did she just make some sort of a change at home?"

I had no idea.

"It feels like there's been a sort of rearranging of things in her house ... not remodeling, but rearranging, redecorating a portion of it ... and it seems as though Susan is very happy about it, because it creates a shift in the energy of things for her mother."

Angie would later confirm that she had recently repainted the interior of her house in a cheerful new color. She seemed delighted to learn that Susan knew all about it.

The evidence that Susan's spirit was present with us mounted as the reading went on. Anne described Susan's sister, painting a highly accurate picture of her personality and present circumstances. She told me about something that Susan liked to wear around her neck that wasn't valuable in a monetary sense, but that was meaningful to her. I recognized this as one of Susan's necklaces that Angie now wore.

"She liked more semiprecious stones, didn't she?" Anne asked. "And I think she must have had quite a collection of them, because I see a little bag with little stones in it. She's showing me that—a little bag with little stones."

I've since learned that in a really good reading, there will be at least one piece of evidence that lets you know beyond a doubt that your loved one is there. That one tidbit, no matter how insignificant it may seem to the medium, will stay with you forever. During my reading with Anne, that little bag of stones was the home run I was hoping for. As I explained to Ann, Susan and Warren's wedding had been a bit nontraditional. A lover of nature, Susan planned an outdoor ceremony. She scattered rose petals to the four directions of the earth, and all in attendance received an enduring gift from nature to take with us as a remembrance of the occasion: a small mesh bag filled with little stones.

At the end of the hour-long reading, I understood why one of Anne's clients had driven into a telephone pole after leaving a session with her. Emotionally drained and dazed, I had to go for a walk to clear my head.

My reading with Anne only intensified my sense of purpose. I dedicated the next year to researching mediumship and writing Anne and Wayne's story. Ty had taken a one-year assignment as a defense contractor, working long hours Monday through Friday. I easily filled the time he was gone with my writing, kept company by our dachshund, Rudy, and his new sister, another long-haired dachshund we named Gretchen.

Always in the back of my mind was Anne's pronouncement that I would unfold mediumistically, and I continued my daily meditation. It was wonderful to be assured of Susan's presence through two gifted mediums, but just as when I'd asked to see her spirit along the mountain trail in Croatia, I still wanted to sense her around me first-hand.

One sunny afternoon about three months into writing Anne's story, I decided to take a break from my computer. I'd been crafting a scene in which Anne reunited a long-lost brother and sister with a little help from their mother in the spirit world. With the images of that loving reunion so vivid in my mind's eye, I moved from my desk in the kitchen to an armchair in the living room and closed my eyes.

I took a few deep breaths and systematically relaxed my body from head to toe. It didn't take long to reach the now-familiar light altered state of meditation.

Susan, I prayed, *please show yourself to me. Come here now and let me know you're around. I would really like to see you.*

I opened my eyes and saw nothing but the familiar walls and furniture of the living room. I tried relaxing my focus and letting my lids droop as I'd seen Anne do, but the scene remained the same.

Resigned to yet another failed attempt, I was about to close my eyes again, when Rudy shot out of his bed and ran into the hallway adjoining the living room where I sat. He stopped three feet short of the front door and stared up as if someone had stepped into the foyer.

Beyond Rudy's unusual behavior, what struck me most at that moment was that Gretchen remained in her bed in the kitchen. Always Rudy's copycat, she mimicked whatever he did, yet she hadn't shown the slightest reaction to whatever it was that had attracted her brother's attention.

I watched, incredulous, when Rudy moved to his left as if following something. He hopped up one step onto the landing at the foot of the stairs. There he stopped and stared up at a framed picture on the wall. It was the black and white portrait of Susan that I had drawn and surrounded with a swarm of yellow butterflies.

I inhaled slowly as I pushed my logical mind aside and allowed magical possibilities in their place. What if Susan were standing there, and she realized the dog could see her? If I were Susan, I'd walk over to my picture, then point at it and say, "Tell her it's me!" Rudy's actions reflected exactly this scenario.

I kept my eyes riveted on Rudy, awestruck, as he now moved from the landing to the living room. He stopped and turned toward the empty chair across from mine. With his head cocked to one side, his face expressed complete confusion. After a moment, he crossed the room, jumped onto the couch, and continued to warily stare at the armchair.

I looked from Rudy to the chair, then said softly to Susan, "You're there, aren't you?"

I heard nothing in reply, but the way Rudy pinned his ears against his head spoke volumes. I might not have been able to see Susan, but that afternoon she let me know in the best way she could that she was with me.

Anne Gehman was the first to explain to me that we live in a world of pulsating energy. Everything that exists vibrates, including us humans. We are immersed in the same sea of energy of which we're made—a sea filled with waves that carry information in their patterns.

We know that radio waves, television and cell phone signals are in the air all around us. We can't tune into them with our physical senses because the vibrations are too high. We need radios, TVs, and cell phones to detect and interpret these imperceptible signals. A medium is able to tune in to the vibration of the discarnate human spirit. According to Anne, it was like tuning the dial on a radio until she picked up a particular frequency. Mediumship was all about attunement.

First Penny, then Anne, and now even my dachshund was able to tune into Susan's spirit. I couldn't see anything but an empty chair, but I thanked Susan for the visit and prayed to see with new sight.

All the world's in vibration,
One big pulsing mass.
This you'll see quite clearly
When from your body you pass.

All things are connected,
Intimately intertwined
By a web of pure love
Which is sewn by the mind.

Once thus linked, always there.
You can access it at will.
This is why those who've passed
Are there with you still.

6

Just Call Me Bill

Even if my father's tolerance for tequila exceeded my own, after two of my mother's margaritas he had to be feeling *something*. As for me, I was now feeling brave enough to raise a subject that had always been taboo in our family: life after death. It wasn't that the afterlife was touchy in and of itself. It's just that a discussion of eternal life might lead to talk of a Creator of some sort, and for reasons that I never understood, our family certainly never talked about *that*.

With no religious guidance from my parents, my concept of God was self-formed. In my younger days, I sometimes felt deprived of the church experiences my schoolmates had. As an adult, I saw this as an unintended blessing. Left to do my own seeking, I had the freedom to try out different beliefs and to discard those that didn't feel right. In the year since Susan died, my changing concept of the nature of reality had caused my concept of God to change as well. I now looked at the world with a new sense of wonder, and increasingly better understood my relationship with God in that world.

I watched my father take another sip of his drink. It wasn't that he'd get angry if I talked about religion. Dad was a gentle, quiet man, but like most of us, he could get fired up if you pushed the right buttons. I hated confrontation more than most, and knew I was about to push a button marked, "Do not touch."

When I'd shared the transcript of the reading with Penny in which Susan had come through so clearly, Dad had dismissed every word of it. In my mind, there was no other way to explain the information Penny had brought through about Susan except that Susan's spirit had given Penny that information. Still, my father had found a way to justify every bit of the mind-boggling evidence in a case that would not have held up in any court.

I could continue the family tradition and keep my mouth shut, but Dad was now ninety-two. I didn't want to delay the discussion any longer. I swirled the ice in my glass, wondering if he was primed enough for me to raise the subject. There was only one way to find out.

"So, Dad," I said, scooting forward to the edge of the couch. "After writing Anne Gehman's story, I'm more convinced than ever that this life is not all there is. I've been sharing the chapters with you . . . have they helped you to see things any differently?"

I watched him warily. He didn't wince. He didn't glance away. In fact, he actually smiled. *Thank you, Jose Cuervo.*

"Well, sweetie, it's a good story," Dad said, "but I don't believe in any of that stuff. As far as I'm concerned, when you die, you die. Death is The Big Sleep. The curtain comes down, and it's just a lot of darkness."

I blew a puff of air through my lips and shook my head. "How depressing."

He shrugged and asked, "Why would I want to live forever?"

I explained that the other side wasn't like it is here in the physical world—that it's far more beautiful, suffused with love, and free of the aging body.

Dad gave me a look that told me he wasn't buying it.

I turned to my mother for support. Normally, she would

share her opinion, except when it came to a talk like this. Now she sat tight-lipped and seemed to deliberately avert her eyes from mine. What had happened to these two to sour them so on all spiritual topics?

I turned back to Dad. "Wouldn't you want to spend eternity with Mom?" After 61 years together, their love was stronger than most couples ever hope for.

He put his hand on Mom's knee and smiled. "Your mother and I have enjoyed every day of our lives together. I couldn't ask for more than that."

I sighed. From what I'd learned of the afterlife, I knew that he could ask for a lot more. I also knew that no amount of tequila was going to change my father's deeply ingrained beliefs. Satisfied that I'd at least broached the subject, I agreed to disagree, but not without a parting shot.

"Dad," I said, "One day I'm going to meet you on the other side. And when I do, I'm going to greet you with a great big hug and say, 'I told you so!'"

He gave me a tolerant smile, and we left it at that.

Shortly after that discussion, Ty and I moved from Northern Virginia to The Villages, Florida, a community where my parents lived just three miles away. After spending the winter in our new house, we decided to head back to sea for an extended cruise. I reluctantly said goodbye to my parents. Dad seemed to be slowing down a lot, and I wasn't happy about leaving. Just three weeks after our departure my mother called me on my cell phone. Dad had suffered a stroke. She didn't know how bad it was. Could I come home right away?

We sailed all night to reach a port in the Florida Keys where we could rent a car. Distraught and distracted, Ty did the driving as I talked to my sister and brother on the phone. They both lived much farther away and asked me to let them know if I felt they needed to fly in.

One look at Dad and my heart sank. I barely recognized the old man lying in the bed. How could he have changed so much in such a short time? Happily, he recognized me, but his speech was slurred and he seemed strangely detached. He didn't seem to know where he was or why everyone was making such a fuss. Always known for his grip of steel, the hand I reached for lay limply in my own.

My mother did her best to stay positive. She told me the doctors said that dad's left side was paralyzed, but that he would slowly regain his abilities. As much as I wanted to believe the doctors, all of my senses told me they were wrong.

I kept my thoughts to myself and stepped into the hallway. I knew my siblings were expecting a call, but I had to make another call first. I pulled up the "favorites" list in my phone and pressed the familiar number. In the year that I'd been working on *The Priest and the Medium*, I'd grown to love Anne and Wayne. Certainly, their experience as pastoral caregivers would be helpful at a time like this, but it was Anne's special skills I needed now.

I exhaled in relief when she answered and told her about my father's stroke.

"What are the doctors saying?" she asked, her soothing voice putting me more at ease than I'd felt all day.

"They say he's going to get better."

"But what do *you* think?"

Her question surprised me, and forced me to face what I was feeling. "I don't think he's going to get better at all," I admitted. In fact, I had a strong feeling that Dad's systems were going to shut down one after another.

Anne made a humming noise, and I knew from experience that she was checking out the situation psychically.

"The doctors don't think it's that bad," I added, "but I think I should tell my sister and brother to come."

Anne hummed again, then said, "I think that would be a good idea."

I sucked in my breath. Anne's comment confirmed what my intuition was telling me. I knew what she was saying; still, I needed to hear it aloud. "Do you think he's going to die?"

She paused, then simply repeated her answer. "I think it would be good for your father to have his family with him right now."

Brent and Janice arrived the next day. They seemed as shocked by Dad's appearance as I'd been. Mom, however, hung her hopes on the second-hand reports now coming from the nurses. We kids had yet to see a doctor.

Dad's family physician didn't have rights in the hospital, so none of us recognized the assigned doctor when he finally made an appearance midday.

"Where do you think he's from?" my brother asked in a whisper.

I didn't think before replying, "Ghana."

Brent gave me a funny look and I mirrored his expression back at him. *Where did that come from?* I'd never met the doctor. Never heard his name. Yes, the man's skin was darker than most African Americans in the area, but that's not why I said what I had. I'd simply *known* the answer.

After examining my father, the doctor met with our family in a private conference room. He remained smiling and positive and did his best to put us at ease. Time would tell us more than he could at that point.

He rose to leave, and as we joined him, I asked the question that wouldn't give me rest: "Doctor," I said, "where are you from?"

He flashed me a pearly smile and replied, "Ghana."

I gave him a "that's nice" nod. Meanwhile, I felt my brother's eyes boring into my back. When I turned to meet them, he stared at me as if I had cooties. What could I do but shrug? This kind of "knowingness" had been happening more and more often lately.

One thing I couldn't know for sure was what was going to happen to my father. Each morning a series of specialists breezed into the room and spoke to us about getting Dad in shape for rehabilitation. The more they smiled, the more agitated I became. My father hadn't eaten in the five days since he'd arrived at the hospital. He could do nothing for himself, and he seemed to be deteriorating mentally, drifting in and out of consciousness. I bugged the nurses about his blood test results, intuitively asking about his kidney function. The numbers were heading in the wrong direction, going from good to bad to worse.

In desperation I called Anne.

"What are the doctors telling you?" she asked.

"They say they're going to send him to rehab."

She sucked in her breath. "How can they say that?"

"That's what I want to know."

"Don't listen to the doctors," Anne advised. "Listen to your intuition, Suzanne."

I shared this with my siblings, but not with my mother, who didn't want to hear bad news of any kind. My sister retreated down the hallway to call her husband, Allan. I knew she was torn about whether to stay a while longer or to go home. She'd now missed almost a week of work and was missing Allan as well.

"Did you decide what to do?" I asked when she came back.

"I'm staying," Janice said.

"Really?"

"Yeah," she nodded. "When I told Allan what you said after your phone call, he said I couldn't ignore you and Anne Gehman."

I blinked in surprise. I could understand his listening to Anne, but to me, as well? Somehow my intuition had gained some credibility of its own.

The next morning, the mood changed. The doctors' smiles turned to frowns as they read the lab reports. I overheard them talking about "renal" this and "cardiac that." Dad's systems seemed to be shutting down, just as I'd felt so strongly they would when I'd first seen him. The word "rehabilitation" was suddenly and irrevocably replaced with a new word: "hospice."

I didn't want to think about the finality represented by that word, but at least we were now speaking honestly about my father's condition. Anxious to escape the grim hospital environment, I offered to check out a facility near our house that the nurses recommended.

When I stepped inside the Cornerstone Hospice, I gave a silent prayer of thanks at finding such an oasis of serenity. By now my father was barely aware of his surroundings. He wouldn't be able to appreciate the soothing atmosphere and loving staff that greeted me, but our family was as much in need of TLC as Dad. I had no idea that such a place existed for people in our situation. Standing in a lobby that looked more like a cozy lodge than a hospital, I was even more surprised to smell the long-forgotten scent of Blue Grass perfume. I had always associated it with my grandmother, and I hadn't smelled it since she'd passed to the other side years earlier.

I returned to the hospital and reported my findings. "It's absolutely perfect," I said, "and it even smells like Grandmom's perfume."

Once we agreed to provide hospice care for Dad, the discharge papers appeared far faster than we'd expected. An unmarked ambulance whisked my father to the new facility while we followed behind, trying to come to terms with the meaning of this final move. My family shuffled about in the lobby while two nurses got Dad settled into a private room. We spoke in hushed tones, relieved to be out of the sterile environment, and amazed at the rapid change of circumstances.

A nurse motioned for us to enter Dad's room. We watched as an aide lovingly tucked a handmade quilt around my father's broken body. The beautiful spread was adorned with colorful butterflies, reminding me of the not-so-subtle signs Susan had sent us in Croatia. I realized now how appropriate the butterfly was as a symbol for those dealing with loss, for just as the caterpillar makes a transition to a more beautiful existence, so, too, does the human spirit after the transition we call death.

Sunlight streamed into Dad's room through French doors that led to a small patio overlooking a sparkling lake. Two sandhill cranes pecked in the grass under a majestic oak nearby. As serious as the moment was, we couldn't help but feel the love and peace in this blessedly tranquil setting.

"This is so much better than the hospital," Janice said softly.

I agreed, then cocked my head and sniffed. "And see? There's Grandmom's perfume." I hadn't sensed it since my earlier visit, but now it once again filled my nostrils.

My sister sniffed, then shook her head. "I don't smell it."

I gaped at her. How could she not? It was unmistakable. Then I remembered something Anne Gehman had told me: that the spirit world often lets people know they are around by recreating a familiar scent, be it the smell of cigar smoke, a favorite flower, or in this case, a special perfume. Nothing identified my grandmother more personally than the scent of Blue Grass.

I suddenly felt lightheaded as I stared at my father. The realization of what was happening was almost overwhelming, but it made perfect sense. My grandmother had reached across dimensions to send me a very clear message when I'd first stepped into the hospice lobby: She approved of this final resting place for her son. Now that we had brought him there, she was communicating with me again in no uncertain terms: She was there to escort her son home.

Two days later, my father, Bill Smeltzer, passed peacefully from this world to the next with his family at his side. Ty and I stayed around for a few weeks to help my mother adjust, then we headed back to Boot Key Harbor. I'd kept myself together fairly well since my father's death, but seeing our boat as we rode the marina launch out to our mooring brought my fragile emotions to the surface.

I couldn't help but recall the phone call from my mother that had started the cascade of recent events. I realized that the last time I'd been aboard *Liberty* I had a father, and now I didn't. I drifted back to our final moments together, when I'd watched the pulse in his neck beat for the last time. The finality of that moment brought a flood of tears and sudden, wracking sobs. Startled, my husband pulled me into his arms and held me tight. He didn't need to ask me what was wrong, but I felt the need to explain.

"I can't believe I'll never see my father again," I cried into his chest.

Ty took hold of both of my shoulders and pushed me away from him so that he could look into my eyes. "Suzanne," he said, "you're the one who taught me that you *will* see your dad again."

I blinked at him as his words sank in. He nodded twice to assure me of the truth in what he'd said.

"You're right," I said, and took in a jagged breath. "I forgot."

"Your dad is still around," Ty said, reaching out to wipe away a tear. "You just can't see him."

I couldn't deny what he said. The transformation in my father's body within minutes of that last heartbeat had stunned me. Anyone who has ever seen a lifeless body knows what I'm talking about. It's not a heartbeat that makes a human being human. Seeing the instant, drastic change in my father's appearance showed me once again that it's the *spirit* that animates the body. Once my father's spirit departed, we were left with just a vessel that no longer even looked like him. My father's spirit, just like Susan's and every other being, could never die. My grief had caused me to temporarily forget the main message of mediumship.

Grief is a necessary process, but Ty's words reminded me that we grieve for ourselves, not for those who have passed. Once I dried my tears, I focused my thoughts on happier times that we had shared and the experience my father was having now, free of his aged body. I couldn't help but wonder what he'd thought when he discovered that there was no final curtain after all.

I didn't have to wait long to find out.

Two months after my father passed, I received an unexpected call from Janet Nohavec telling me that she had an opening for a reading the following Wednesday. I'd been on her waiting list since I'd met her through Anne months earlier, but had put all thoughts of a reading aside. When I'd initially asked to sit with Janet, I only wanted to hear from my stepdaughter, Susan. Now I realized this was a chance to connect with my father as well.

Separated by several states, Janet conducted my reading by phone. At first I had doubts that she could bring through anything meaningful without being in the same room with me. Janet quickly demonstrated that a medium connects with the energy of the spirit and doesn't need to be present with the sitter.

"There's a gentleman here who was pretty sick," she said. "Who would have worked around coal?"

I couldn't believe it. I often bragged to friends that in my father's early days with the Pennsylvania railroad, he'd shoveled coal on the big steam locomotives. I passed this information on to Janet.

Pleased, she went on to prove herself as an evidential medium by revealing details about my father's long-standing heart condition and his feelings toward me. She then made mention of some kind of naval connection. I thought back to the dinner shared with Anne and Wayne the year before. As far as I could recall, I hadn't mentioned my background as a naval officer.

"Was this pretty recent?" Janet asked, "because this is not an old passing. It feels pretty recent. And there's something about Bill . . . ."

"That was his name," I confirmed, wiping my tears.

"Did you write some kind of poem or a letter at the end?"

I laughed now with joy. "My brother did! It was a tribute to my dad, and it was so good that my mother had it framed for all of us." A copy hung on the wall of our study.

"Well," Janet said, "he's acknowledging that that poem is very, very important to him."

I squeezed my eyes shut, acutely aware of Janet's use of the present tense. She could not have known about that poem, but she was clearly showing me that my father knew about the verses my brother wrote *after* Dad passed.

I knew then that what mediums had been saying for over a century was true: Our loved ones are around us after they cross to the other side. They read our poems—yes—but according to Janet, that wasn't all.

"Your mother must be talking to a picture of him, because I'm supposed to tell her that he hears her all the time. I don't know if she put his ring on or she's holding his ring, but it's very significant to him. He brought that up."

It was true: my mother had been wearing Dad's wedding ring next to her own since he passed, and she had recently told me that she talked to his picture quite often. Mom admitted that she felt a little silly doing so, but I planned to set her straight about that as soon as I got off the phone.

With stunning accuracy, Janet gave additional evidence about my father, then she shifted gears and brought in a new presence.

"Your dad's talking about someone else who died tragically who wasn't that old, and I feel quickness with this passing. Why do I have to go back a couple of years?"

I held my breath and explained that my stepdaughter had been killed two years ago—another fact I'd kept from Janet at our initial meeting.

"Why was there some delay when she died?" Janet asked. "Some delay about someone finding out? Delay . . . delay . . . ."

I thought back to the remote island in Croatia where we'd been when we got the news. Susan had been gone two days before the family found us.

I shared this with Janet, and she went on to give me details as fast as I could write them down. She alternated with evidence from Susan and my father, talking more with them than with me, saying words like, "Give that to me again" and "Say it another way," that let me know it wasn't just Janet and me in this unusual conversation between two worlds.

Janet's fire-hose flow of meaningful information left me weak and shaky, but excited. Ty and Angie would be thrilled to get new information from Susan, and my own mother would not be able to deny that Dad was still around.

Janet began to wrap things up by asking if I had any questions. There was only one thing I wanted to know.

"Please ask my Dad if he's surprised that there's more."

There was a brief silence on the other end, then Janet replied, "He says it was like an 'aha' moment, so I don't know that I would say 'surprised.'" She paused again, then added, "It's almost like he feels contentment."

And that's exactly what I felt when I hung up the phone: sheer contentment.

I passed along Dad's messages to my brother and sister, but most especially to my mother. Back when we'd sipped those margaritas and had our discussion about life after death, I sensed that she wanted to believe, but after 61 years with my dad, their beliefs, like their lives, had almost become one. The fact that she'd been talking to Dad since he passed showed me that she wanted very much to believe he might hear her.

She listened with tear-filled eyes as I read the notes from the reading. When I typed them on paper and gave her a copy, she read them several times. Her energy increased dramatically in the days after that reading with Janet. She had a spring in her step that none of us had seen in quite a while.

"I feel more at peace than I have since your father died," Mom told me.

And that, I knew, was the whole point of consulting a medium. That may also be why she agreed to go with me for a first-hand experience of her own with a medium. I'd heard about a woman in our community named Maria who gave readings, but that's all I knew. I had no idea what kind of medium she was. How good was her connection with the spirit world? Was she clairvoyant, clairaudient, clairsentient, or all three? Would she give airy-fairy messages or hard-core evidence?

I no longer needed to have anything proven to me, but my mother was a different story. Would Maria leave my mother feeling conned or convinced? What if she didn't connect with my father? Would she lose that spring in her step? I had to take the risk.

When Mom and I walked into Maria's home, I felt as nervous as I had before my own first reading. Penny had changed my life that day, and I prayed that Maria would do the same for my mother. Just like Penny, Maria only read for one person at a time. She disappeared with my mother into a back room, leaving me to leaf aimlessly through magazines on the coffee table.

I sprang to attention like a midshipman when the two of them emerged an hour later. There was no time to ask my mother how it went before Maria whisked me into the back room for my turn. My mother's face had told me nothing. What had Maria said? She began the reading without pre-amble. Her first words answered any questions I might have asked.

"I'm hearing one word over and over," she said, "Dad, Dad, Dad, Dad, Dad, and I gave your mom a name that I have to give to you now: *Bill*. He won't leave."

I wanted to jump up and hug her. "You told my mom that? You told her *Bill* was here?"

"Yes," she said matter-of-factly. "I told her that he said to just call him Bill."

I fell back against the chair and went limp. Few people knew that my father's real name was Oliver, but for some reason he'd always gone by his nickname. If people somehow learned his real name first, he always used those exact four words to let them know what to call him: *Just call me Bill*.

"You said that to my mother? 'Just call me Bill?'" I could barely breathe.

"Yes," Maria said, unaware of the enormity of her words. "And now he's giving you big bear hugs. You're being squeezed to pieces."

I laughed with happiness. My father's exuberance often resulted in hugs that left me as breathless as I felt now.

"He's a new spirit," Maria said. "He's meeting people on the other side. He says, 'I've met up with my brother.'"

Dad's brother had passed just after he did.

"He's moving around well and he pats his chest and says, 'It's okay here, too.'"

More awesome confirmation. I couldn't wait to compare notes with my mother.

We did just that over a cup of coffee in a nearby sandwich shop when my reading was over. We had to stop, because I was too shaken to drive any farther. I learned that Maria had done even better than I'd thought. She'd relayed information about Dad's German heritage and his difficulty getting around before he passed. Best of all was a statement from Dad that he'd "heard the whistle blow, and knew it was time to go."

That message from a retired railroad engineer could not have been more perfect. Equally comforting was the affirmation that my father had been aware of his family at his bedside when he took his last breath.

My mother was now convinced beyond a doubt that she hadn't lost her husband forever, but it was Maria's final message for me that made the reading so memorable. My coffee mug trembled in my hand as I described to my mother the surprising grand finale to the afternoon's session.

My hour with Maria had been nearing its end, and I realized I hadn't yet heard from the one spirit who I always longed to hear from.

"Is there a young woman here?" I'd asked, feeling as if I were somehow cheating by prompting her.

"Why, yes," Maria had answered, waving a hand as if in dismissal. "She's been here all along, but she keeps using your name, saying, 'I'm Susan! I'm Susan!'"

I gasped in disbelief at how I almost hadn't mentioned her. "She's not giving you *my* name. I'm *Suzanne*. Susan is the one I'm looking for." It was the most honest mistake I could imagine.

"Oh, well, *Susan* is here," Maria said, "and she's so bubbly, and happy, and alive."

After everything Maria had said to that point, that accurate description of our Susan would have been enough for me. But then—with one last sentence that left me a sobbing mess—Maria put the final stamp of approval on her abilities and validated everything I'd come to believe about life after death:

"This young girl?" Maria said, "This Susan? Well, she's telling me that she's filling your life with butterflies."

So many wish to know
What heaven's really like.
Are there truly flowers,
Harps and music, and the like?

Heaven is your self-same world.
We live right here beside you.
The difference lies in the love we feel.
Its presence ever does abide you.

In this world of thought,
Where no matter does exist,
Surrounded are we all by Love
Whose great force we can't resist.

Because of all the energy
Of which we are a part,
We feel the love more strongly here,
Like a pulsing, beating heart.

Our world is very real to us
As real as yours to you.
And if we wish to do something
We need only think it through.

For thought is our creator.
We travel with the mind.
We maintain our connection thus
With those to whom our love does bind.

In a realm of such great love
One truly does find peace.
And so you will find heaven
When earth's bonds you do release.

Just know that love's eternal –
A continuation of the soul.
Whether there or here you travel
It is love that keeps you whole.

7

Attunement

I felt like a different person the week I spent in Lily Dale, New York, interviewing Anne and Wayne for their book. The inner glow I experienced came from being immersed in the high spiritual energy that had built up there over the Spiritualist community's long history. A sense of peace pervades the wooded streets along the shores of Cassadaga Lake, and the glow stayed with me for days after I left. That kind of feeling is hard to come by, and I longed to go back.

My excuse to return came in the form of an unexpected phone call from Janet Nohavec just a short time after my reading with her. When Janet identified herself, I couldn't imagine why she was calling me again. It turned out to be a phone call that would point my life in a direction I never expected.

"I know you just finished writing Anne and Wayne's story," Janet said, "and I'm sure you're ready for a break . . . ."

Was I ever. As much as I enjoyed writing, it felt good to have completed such a large, time-consuming project. I'd only recently shipped the manuscript to my agent and was enjoying the freedom of having nothing hanging over my head. It seemed, however, that I was not meant to be idle for long.

"I've been looking for someone to tell my story," Janet continued, "and I was wondering if you'd be willing to do it."

I couldn't help but laugh. *So much for a break.* I'd heard just enough of Janet's story to know that this was another one of those opportunities that writers pray for. I knew first-hand that Janet was an exceptional medium. I also knew that we had a "hook" for her book without even trying: Janet Nohavec, medium and pastor of her own Spiritualist church, had spent four years as a Roman Catholic nun.

That in itself would be interesting to readers, but Janet's childhood was filled with the kind of drama that hooked people on soap operas. The daughter of an abusive, alcoholic father, Janet had battled her own share of demons growing up. Unlike Anne Gehman, who came across as angelic as the spirits she communicated with, Janet was tough, street-smart, and sassy—the least likely nun, medium, or minister I could imagine.

Thinking of nuns reminded me of the reading my mother and I had had with Maria. Along with all the evidence from my father and Susan, Maria had told me some things about myself. Most were quite accurate, but one detail—that I had a group of Catholic sisters guiding me—I attributed to my writing project about a priest married to a medium. Now I couldn't help but wonder if those nuns in the spirit world had a different agenda.

I took a deep breath as Janet waited for my answer. If I agreed to write her story, the project would dominate the next year of my life. Then again, spreading the message of mediumship was not only my mission, but it had become my personal passion. What could I do but laugh and say yes?

So, less than eleven months since my first visit to Lily Dale, I found myself back in that haven of happiness. Were it not for mediums such as Janet Nohavec and Anne Gehman, I would have shied away from writing about a topic that had such potential for criticism, but Janet and Anne were the real deal. As different as they were in style and personality, each brought dignity and integrity to her work. Janet owned a large summer getaway three doors down from Anne and Wayne's pink and white cottage. Owners of two of the most sought-after lots in the community, they shared the same idyllic, unobstructed view of Cassadaga Lake.

This would be Round Two of my interviews with Janet. The first had taken place at my sister's house, halfway between my home and Janet's church in northern New Jersey. I'd learned then all I needed to get started writing about her childhood. This visit to Lily Dale was a chance to observe Janet in action, not just as a medium, but as a teacher of mediumship. My research into her life wouldn't be complete without knowing what her teaching style was like and what kind of things she taught her students.

The two of us dodged potholes on the short walk from her house to the classroom at Lily Dale's Lakeside Assembly Hall. A full day of rain had left the dirt and gravel road a muddy mess.

"Listen, Janet," I said as I sidestepped a puddle, "I don't want any of the students to know I'm there to write your story. Just ignore me, and I'll do my best to blend in with everyone else."

"Oh, no." Janet waved a dismissive hand. "You're going to have your own experience this weekend."

Potholes or not, my eyes left the road and fixed on her face. "What do you mean?"

"You're going to have an experience with Spirit."

"How do you know?" I asked, shocked, but excited at the prospect.

Janet tilted her head and gave me a look that clearly said, *You ought to know better than to ask me that.*

I shrugged sheepishly and said, "Oh yeah—you're a psychic medium."

Once inside the classroom, I slipped into a chair in the third row while Janet organized her paperwork at the podium. Truth be told, I was thrilled for this excuse to learn the actual how-to's of mediumship. Until now a mere consumer of what I had previously considered a gift and not a skill, I was anxious to find out how to develop the abilities of a medium. I'd always assumed that one had to have been aware of the spirit world from childhood. That certainly held true with Anne Gehman and Janet Nohavec.

Could I possibly make contact with the spirit world, myself? Was something going to happen in class, as Janet said? I slowly scanned the assembly hall. Built in the 1880s, the main room was large and open, with plain white paint. Framed black and white photos of some of the greatest mediums in the history of Spiritualism adorned the walls. At what age had each of them first become aware of the presence of the spirit world? I didn't know, but I allowed myself to hope that a person didn't have to be a born medium to make contact with the other side.

When Janet began speaking, I surreptitiously turned on my tape recorder. After a few introductory remarks, she took a seat next to the podium and began to lead the class through a meditation. I left the recorder running in order to capture Janet's phraseology. I knew the wording would make good material for her biography, but I was happy to have the recording for myself as well. In light of her announcement that I would have my own experience during the class, everything related to Janet's work held a new and personal fascination.

When Janet returned to the podium and began the first lecture, I hung on every word. Janet explained mediumship that day in a way that caused me to view the spirit world in a new light. She told the class that the spirit people were as anxious to speak with us as we were with them. This, I liked. It meant that mediums served not only their client, but they served the spirit world just as much. Janet painted a happy picture of those in spirit rejoicing when they find a new medium. What better way for the unseen world to let their loved ones on earth know they're okay?

According to Janet, the more mediums standardized their systems for connecting with the other side, the easier it was for both sides to communicate. I had never thought of spirits as being intelligent and willing to use specific processes to work with a medium, but why wouldn't they be? Janet handed out worksheets with a list of the information students should expect to receive from the spirits they linked in with. The list included such items as "Was the spirit old or young when they died? Male or female? How did they die? Was it from a sudden event or from an illness? What kind of work did they do? What was their relationship with the sitter?"

Janet told the class to memorize the list and to set a clear intention with the spirit world that they wanted to receive the items on the page every time they gave a reading—a kind of name, rank, and serial number checklist. I loved how this concept emphasized that mediumship was a cooperative relationship between the two realms of existence. Best of all, it allowed me to use my linear, military mind in the preparation phase before surrendering to the more passive, receptive state that Janet said was so vital for attuning with the spirit world.

Janet stepped out from behind the podium. "Okay, that's enough talking for me," she said with her hands on her hips. "It's time to put what we've covered so far into practice. I want someone to come up here and try to get 'name, rank, and serial number.'"

This is going to be good, I thought. Janet had told me before class that several of those who'd signed up were practicing mediums in their hometowns. Maybe one of them would bring through Susan or my dad. I looked at the students around me. Experienced or not, nobody raised their hand to go first.

"Come on. Who's it gonna be?" Janet asked, then without pause, said, "How about you, Suzanne?"

My jaw dropped and I choked out a small laugh. *Was she kidding?* Her smug expression told me she was not. I wanted nothing more than to exercise my choice to decline, but how could I say no after her earlier prediction? The pull of gravity seemed particularly strong as I reluctantly rose from my chair and walked the endless distance to the front of the class. When I turned and faced the students, their smiles of encouragement meant little. To me they felt like a firing squad, capable of inflicting death by humiliation.

I felt I had more of a chance of pulling a rabbit out of a hat than bringing through a spirit on demand. I wanted to run out the door and tell Janet to find someone else to write her book. Then I noticed that she, too, was smiling. I recalled from our long hours of interviews how her teachers in England had pushed and stretched her far beyond her comfort zone, but always for the purpose of making her the best medium possible. I knew by now that Janet came from the heart in everything she did. She would never put me on the spot if she didn't know what she was doing. All I could do was trust her.

"Okay, so what do I do?" I asked, resigned to my fate and anxious to get it over with.

"Close your eyes and ask for the loved one of someone in the room to come and stand behind you."

I happily closed my eyes. That way I couldn't see everyone looking at me. The real challenge was figuring out what to do with my arms. If I crossed them over my chest, I'd look defensive. If I hung them straight down at my side, I'd feel awkward and vulnerable. Then I remembered what Janet had said about serving the spirit world. This wasn't about me at all. I closed my eyes and chose awkward and vulnerable.

I pushed aside the thought of failure and silently invited the relative of someone in the classroom to step behind me. After what seemed like an interminable period of silence, Janet said, "Okay, so what do you feel?"

I shook my head. "I don't feel anything."

"Don't try so hard," she said. "There's someone standing with you, so just try to sense, is it a male or female?"

My eyes shot open and locked on Janet's. *There was a spirit behind me?* I hadn't known Janet long, but I knew her well enough to know that she would neither lie nor make up a story. She was a phenomenal medium who could see, hear, and sense the spirit world with ease. If she said there was someone there, then there was a glimmer of hope that I might actually be able to tune in to them.

I closed my eyes and tried to relax. Male or female? Male or female? *How was I supposed to know?* I reminded myself not to think so much and allowed myself to simply feel.

I didn't feel much of anything, but I knew I had to say something. "It's a man," I said, waiting for the first volley from the firing squad.

"That's right," Janet said.

The corner of my mouth went up, but I kept my thoughts to myself. *Let's hear it for fifty-fifty odds.*

"Okay, did he die old or young?"

I took a deep breath. *Help me out here,* I prayed, then suddenly I heard the number 70. It was fast and fleeting, and the voice sounded the same as my thoughts. Surely I'd imagined it, but everyone was waiting for me to say something, so I said, "He was older. Seventy years old."

"Very good," Janet said. "Now remember: 'name, rank, and serial number.' Ask him to tell you what he died from."

And just like that, I knew the man had died of cancer. I knew it just as I had known that my father's doctor was from

Ghana. It made no sense; I simply knew.

"He died of cancer," I said, not bothering to open my eyes.

"Okay. Good. Now find out what he did for a living."

I reminded myself to breathe, and I waited, aware that Janet hadn't yet denied anything I'd said.

"You're stiff as a board," she interjected. "Relax and just know that he's there."

I felt about as relaxed as a robot. Okay, I said to the spirit that was allegedly standing behind me, What kind of work did you do? I waited again, and then, another fleeting word passed through my mind.

"I heard 'engineer,'" I said, surprised.

"Excellent," Janet said, then she turned to the class. "We have a male here from the spirit world who died of cancer at age 70, and he was an engineer. Can anyone take this so far?"

I opened my eyes and scanned the students. One side of my brain scoffed and the other begged for someone to identify what I'd said.

A woman in the back row raised her hand and said, "I can."

I gaped at her, beyond grateful for this stay of execution.

"What can you take?" Janet asked.

"All of it," she said. "My father passed at age 70. He had cancer, and he was an engineer."

I swear I felt the earth move.

"That's outstanding," Janet said, and gave me a proud I-told-you-so smile.

The other students murmured and nodded. I stood there trying to figure the odds of getting four pieces of evidence right. At this point, basic math was beyond me.

As if unaware of the battle taking place between my left brain and right, Janet proceeded to have her own conversation with the woman.

"Your dad had a really good sense of humor, didn't he? Because he's joking around now and telling me how you two used to see who could make the other laugh hardest."

"That's right," the woman nodded, smiling at the memory.

"And he's telling me he used to like to work with his hands, and he's showing me these ball caps that he used to collect."

The woman nodded again. "Yes, he did."

I knew now that Janet was right there beside me, and that she wasn't going to let me fall. A wave of gratitude flooded my chest. By linking in and bringing through those small but evidential details about the man, she proved to me that his spirit was really there. Without her I would have forever wondered if I had simply made up the details I provided.

"See what else you can get about him," Janet prompted.

I sighed and fidgeted. I had thought my turn was over. As uncomfortable as I was, curiosity overcame my discomfort. Could I keep this link going? I closed my eyes again and stood like a mannequin. It felt foreign, waiting for something to happen, *anything at all*, a word, a picture, a sound . . . .

And then the reward: words came that had no reason to pop into my mind unless some outside source had placed them there.

"I sense that this man must have liked dancing," I said, "because I just heard the word 'foxtrot' and then—" I laughed at the absurdity, '—I see a pair of patent leather shoes and I heard the word 'twinkletoes!'"

Janet and I turned in unison to the back row for confirmation. When I saw the woman's broad smile, my heart soared.

"He and my mother loved to dance," she said. "Twinkletoes was his nickname."

"*Really?*" I said, incredulous.

Janet clapped her hands like a kid.

It seemed too good to be true. Cancer, I might have guessed. A seventy-year-old man could have been a coincidence and plenty of men were engineers, but *Twinkletoes*? That was no product of my imagination.

I wanted to quit while I was ahead, but Janet wasn't having it. "Get some more," she ordered.

Back in mannequin mode, I saw the fleeting image of a tall man with white hair. This and the patent leather shoes were my first taste of clairvoyance. The woman confirmed that the description matched her father. I waited some more, then sensed that he had lived in the country and enjoyed a drink or two. Right again on both counts.

"What else?" Janet asked.

Enough was enough. "I've had about all the fun I can handle for one day," I said, letting my shoulders sag. "May I sit down now, *please?*"

The class broke into laughter, but Janet laughed hardest of all, showing that she understood the limits of discomfort.

Back in my seat, my mind continued to race. I had done it—I'd brought through verifiable and meaningful evidence from a man in spirit, and all of it accurate. It was the last thing I ever expected to do, and I know now that it wouldn't have happened had Janet not planted the seed of possibility in my mind. A person can have all the desire in the world to do something, but belief is the critical ingredient for success.

That evening after class, Janet and I sat in twin rocking chairs on her porch overlooking the lake. She assured me that once the link with spirit was made, it couldn't be broken. In fact, she claimed, it would only get better.

Armed with that dose of confidence, I eagerly practiced the classroom exercises during the rest of the workshop. Whether one-on-one or in small groups, I continued to surprised myself by bringing through accurate details for my classmates about their loved ones who had passed. The pad of paper I'd brought to take notes about Janet's teaching style filled with just as many personal notes as I began to build a list of the evidence I gleaned from the other side: about the stern 80-year-old grandmother with heart problems who spoke German and had a crucifix hanging on her wall; about the loving 60-year-old father who ran a farm and died very suddenly; and about the 50 year-old-uncle who lived in a desert in the Middle East and sat on colorful carpets surrounded by his nieces and nephews . . . .

This kind of detail brought me back to attend Janet's second and third weekend workshops. By then I had finished writing her book and attended purely as a student. Each time I gave a reading to a fellow classmate or stood before the group to get a link I gained more confidence. It was becoming unmistakably clear that the details I was bringing through were no fluke. Could I possibly do this for others outside of a classroom setting? If so, I could share the message of mediumship in a much more convincing way than through my writing.

Still, I had my doubts.

"I feel like I'm making these things up," I told Janet as we sat on her porch in what had become a familiar after-class routine. "The thing is, I'm right more times than I'm wrong, and a lot of the details that are right are really unusual."

Janet shook her head. "You're the most skeptical person I know."

"I take that as a compliment," I said. To me, being skeptical was far better than being gullible.

The problem was that I felt as if I were pulling data out of the air rather than communicating with an actual soul. I might have been linking with the spirit world, but I felt no human connection at all. I shared my concerns with Janet, and she repeated her assertion that the link would improve with time.

I frowned. Janet's workshops were over. I wasn't yet at a point where I felt confident giving readings, so how was I going to improve?

"If I'm going to get any better at this," I told her, "I need to take it seriously. I can't just do this halfway."

We stared at the lake in silence for a few minutes, then I allowed myself to voice a thought that had been playing around in my mind for months.

"Now that I've learned from you," I said, "there's only one other place I'd want to study."

Janet raised her eyebrows. She didn't need to be a psychic to know what place I was talking about. We'd spent hours discussing her training. As good as she was when she first started working as a medium, she found that the British mediums were even better. She had pushed herself beyond her fear of flying and traveled to England to study with the very best.

There was a twinkle in her eyes when she said, "You're thinking of going to Stansted?"

The Arthur Findlay College of Psychic Sciences in Stansted, England, was world renowned for the quality of its teaching. Janet was one of only two overseas teachers approved to teach at the school.

"I'd like to," I said.

She tossed back her head and whistled, then she grew serious and looked me in the eye. "Let me pick out the teachers. You only want the best, but I'm warning you—it's going to be a life-changing experience."

I nodded thoughtfully. My stepdaughter's death had been a life-changing experience. I'd prayed to find proof that Susan's spirit still existed, and I'd found that proof through mediumship. Since then I'd been repeating the same prayer every day to God and the spirit world: *Transform my life. Guide me and show me how I may serve.*

It seemed as if my prayers were being heard.

When things they seem to go just right,
It's because you're in the flow—
Allowing things to just unfold
The way they're supposed to go.

How to know which way is right?
You simply need relax.
Follow your intuition—
Your brain you need not tax.

That subtle inner guidance
Will tell you when and where to turn.
You'll find such peace and freedom
When to follow it you learn.

Go with the flow: such good advice.
Your whole life these words can change
When you find that you need struggle not
Your life to rearrange.

Just trust that you are in good hands
Being guided all the way.
Your prayers are answered perfectly
If you only take the time to pray.

8

Answered Prayers

Since the beginning of my marriage, I had had the same recurring nightmare. In my dream, I was enjoying life with Ty, when I got a phone call from my old college. An administrator would tell me that there'd been a mistake—that I hadn't finished all the requirements for the degree I thought I'd earned years ago. The next thing I knew, I was back living in my old dorm with a roommate half my age. I was miles from the man I love, and the only way I could call home was via a single pay phone in the hallway.

If I had known that dream would be a preview of my experience at Arthur Findlay College, I'm not so sure I would have gone.

There I was—an hour outside of London, thousands of miles from home. I'd said goodbye to my husband two days prior and put away my useless cell phone. Befuddled from jetlag and a series of planes, trains, and buses, I stumbled with my luggage down a dim corridor of Stansted Hall until I found my assigned room. It was just down the hallway from the school's sole pay phone.

I held the long, heavy brass key I'd been issued, but the room's door was ajar. I pushed it open and took in the scene: The small space was longer than it was wide, with a low, angled ceiling that followed the contours of one of the building's many gables. Along the left side of the room stood a small chest of drawers. Atop the dresser sat a tray with a white electric teapot, three white cups and saucers, and a white porcelain bowl filled with tea bags. A stand-alone sink with exposed pipes jutted out from the wall halfway to the lone window at the far end of the room.

Three twin beds arranged like those in a hospital ward lined the right wall. The beds were smaller than standard American size, and the one closest to me was unmade, exposing a gray-and-white striped mattress. The two farthest beds had been made up with maroon spreads that were littered with toiletries and piles of clothes. Upon my entry, the owners of these belongings—two blonde beauties half my age—stopped their unpacking and looked up.

I had to bite my lip to keep from blurting out, *"My God, it's my nightmare come true!"*

I greeted my roommates and learned they hailed from Denmark. Luckily, their English was far better than my Danish, and we exchanged the standard getting-to-know-you questions and answers. Because I was the last to arrive, all of the drawers had been taken, so I busied myself putting my clothes on some shelves in the room's one small closet.

I picked up a flat sheet from the wooden chair by the bed and spread it over the mattress. I tucked the ends tightly at the corners just as I'd been taught at Officers Candidate School. As I did so, I recalled a conversation I'd overheard in the parking lot between a couple as I arrived at the college. The woman had just left the building. As the man helped her load her luggage in his car, he asked how the week of classes had gone.

"It was great," the woman said, "but this place is like boot camp for mediums."

One look at the class schedule proved the woman's analogy quite accurate. Except for meals and a daily break for tea, the hours were filled from just after breakfast until well after dinner each day with lectures for the full group of eighty students, smaller hands-on sessions for more intimate groups of ten to thirty, and periods of guided meditation. If I wanted to have a daily jog, reveille would have to be at dawn.

With my bedspread tight enough to bounce a quarter on, the first order of business was to fill out a questionnaire. The mediumistic experience I listed on the form would be used to determine which of the six teachers I would have for small group work. Janet had filled me in on the tutors who would be leading the week. All were outstanding, and four of the six had visited her church in New Jersey to give demonstrations of mediumship. One, however, stood above the rest in reputation. Mavis Pittilla, according to Janet, was the Grande Dame of mediumship in England.

When I first told Janet I wanted to go to Stansted, we'd sat at her computer and browsed through the college's schedule on the Internet. The school had no resident teachers. Instead, they offered week-long courses year-round, each organized and taught by different groups of approved tutors. Janet wanted to make sure I chose a week with the best possible instructors. The course organizer, Simon James—a brilliant British medium who now lived and worked in Canada—and Mavis Pittilla were the reasons she had recommended this week for me.

I knew I couldn't go wrong with any of the instructors, but to work up close and personally with the best of the best would make the trip all the more special. As I filled out the questionnaire, I worried that I lacked the experience to be in with the teachers I truly wanted—either Simon or Mavis. With only classroom experience to my name, I'd asked Janet to put in a good word for me with her British colleagues. There was no guarantee I would get one of the teachers I most wanted for the small group sessions. As I got to the bottom of the page, I realized it really didn't matter; whatever was meant to happen that week would happen. With the form complete, I headed downstairs to hand it in and have my first look around.

The Arthur Findlay College was named after its benefactor. Arthur Findlay was a British accountant and stockbroker who didn't initially give much credence to Spiritualism. After being exposed to direct evidence of the continuity of life through a gifted medium named John Sloan, Findlay spent five years studying Sloan's work. He became so convinced that the spirit world was real, that he dedicated the rest of his life to spreading the word. He authored several books that became classics in the annals of Spiritualism. His dream was to establish a school for the psychic sciences, and he bequeathed his estate to the Spiritualists' National Union for that purpose.

The main building of the college was Findlay's home, but it was more the size of a large luxury hotel than any private home I'd ever seen. The second and third floors had obviously been remodeled to include dormitory-style rooms and multiple bathrooms, but the main floor still reflected the grandeur of the original estate. A wide staircase led from two ends of the hallway outside my room to a landing, then continued as one wide set of steps into a grand entry hall. I explored the rooms off the main hall and found a library, a formal dining room, and a large sitting room, all of which were now used for classrooms.

Dark walls and heavy furniture gave the college a stately, opulent feel. Ornate carpets adorned the shiny wood floors and thick, brocaded drapes hung over floor-to-ceiling windows. Obviously, Arthur Findlay had invested well. Through the windows I could see a rectangular garden covering several acres, with benches around the perimeter. Horses in heavy wool coats grazed in a field on the far side of a split rail fence. Smaller buildings built from the same red bricks as the manor house sat at the end of a paved path that was adorned with picturesque grape arbors.

I followed handwritten signs to the Blue Room, where a thin man in jeans and a black t-shirt stood collecting questionnaires. This, I learned, was the famous Simon James. I handed in my questionnaire and introduced myself as Janet Nohavec's biographer. If she'd sent him an email about my attendance in his course, he gave no indication of it.

I wanted to talk more with Simon, but he was obviously the man of the hour. The air buzzed with the excitement of the students around me, many of whom greeted each like long-lost friends. I stepped back into the hallway, and it was my turn to exchange hugs. There, before me, stood two familiar faces in a sea of foreigners. Janis Murphy and Claire VanCott were fellow Floridians. Both had attended Janet's classes in Lily Dale with me, and both clearly stood out for the level of their abilities. Claire, a former stockbroker, and Janis, a realtor, proved that there is no stereotypical image of a medium.

It was time to eat, so we wound our way through the maze of hallways to a large, fluorescent-lit, institutional dining room that seemed oddly out of place in the formal manor. We chattered excitedly about our experiences on the journey to England as we filled our plates at a buffet line. We found three seats at a rectangular table with another medium who again defied the stereotypes—a beefy black man named Harold who hailed from Ft. Lauderdale. The Florida contingent happily shared our first impressions of the school as we dug into our meals. At the surrounding tables our fellow students did the same in Dutch, German, French, Danish, or thick British accents.

"Did any of you check out the bathrooms yet?" Harold asked. "They have clawfoot tubs."

A woman leaned in from the next table and said, "You can find a shower if you look hard enough."

"I tried one of the tubs," said Claire. "A young spirit boy came in while I was bathing."

I did a doubletake. "You saw a spirit? While you were in the bathtub?"

"Yeah." She shrugged her shoulders as if it were the most natural thing in the world.

"What did you do?"

"I thanked him for being there, then told him to get the heck out of the bathroom."

I shook my head and laughed. Claire was always good for a laugh, even when she wasn't trying. She'd grown up on Staten Island and held her own working right alongside the good old boys of Wall Street. Nothing fazed her. Her wit was as sharp as her mind, and she had a good heart, balanced always by an unmistakable don't-mess-with-me glint in her eyes.

She went on to describe how she had gotten dressed after her bath and went downstairs, only to see the spirit of an older gentleman walking down the main staircase behind her. His clothing looked like that of a caretaker from a different era, so she'd gone to the front desk and inquired about him.

"I figured those ladies out there have heard it all," she said, "so I described the old guy to them. They said students see him walking around here all the time. Seems he used to take care of the place and doesn't want to leave."

As I listened to Claire's experience, a feeling of happiness and gratitude welled up inside me like a geyser that threatened to erupt. This was a dream situation for me—to be surrounded by people who not only believed in spirits, but saw them with their own eyes, people who didn't fear what others called ghosts, but who understood and respected the spirit world.

This is why I had come—to immerse myself in classes and conversations about the other side, and to increase my ability to tune into that dimension. I envied Claire and those like her who could actually see those in spirit. Hearing her story only intensified my longing to achieve my goals for the week. More than anything, I wanted to trust what I was sensing when I tuned in to my non-physical senses. I wanted to know beyond a doubt that I was connecting with an actual being, not just pulling information out of some cosmic databank.

When the meal was over, my friends and I stepped into the hallway. A crowd had gathered in front of a bulletin board across from the Blue Room. I knew immediately that the small group assignments had been posted. We stepped to the back of the pack and slowly worked our way toward six sheets of paper tacked to the wall. When we got to the front, I scanned across the lists until I came to the one with "Mavis Pittilla" written across the top. My eyes shifted direction and moved quickly down the names of the nine students assigned to her. When I came to number seven, I had no need to look any farther. I threw back my head and let loose a little of the geyser's steam in a silent *Yessssssssssssss!*

A slower scan of the list revealed that of the seven women and two men, I was the only American. I felt bad that neither Claire nor Janis had been chosen for the group, and hoped they would be happy with their assigned tutors. I stepped out of the crowd and stood off to the side until they joined me. Claire had been assigned to Simon James, the course organizer. Janis was in a group led by a woman that none of us knew. We did recall that Janet Nohavec had invited her to speak and demonstrate mediumship at her church in New Jersey, so how bad could she be?

I couldn't help but wonder if Janet had made a petition on my behalf. I excused myself from my friends and found my way to the pay phone on the second floor. I dug Janet's phone number and my international calling card out of my pocket and punched in the long series of digits. As I listened to the phone ring I felt a moment of panic when I remembered the time change. I checked my watch and relaxed. The sun had been up for a few hours back in the States.

By this time in our relationship, Janet knew my voice without introduction, so I wasted no time when she picked up.

"Janet!"

"Hey! Are you in Stansted?"

"I'm here, and guess what?"

"What?"

"I got Mavis Pittilla!"

"You're in Mavis's group?"

"I am!"

You would have thought the Publishers' Clearinghouse Prize Patrol had just told her she'd won a million bucks. Her squealing went on and on in bursts of enthusiasm that left me bent over with laughter.

"You are going to have such a good week!" she said when she finally produced a real sentence.

"Did you have anything to do with this?" I asked.

"I sent an email to Simon asking if he could place you with Mavis, and it looks like he was able to do that."

"Then I'm indebted to both of you, but what if I can't keep up with the group? She's supposed to teach the more advanced students, and I've never actually worked as a medium."

Janet's voice took on a soothing tone. "Don't worry about it. You'll do fine. Just listen to everything she says. You couldn't ask for a better teacher."

We chatted for a few minutes about the school, then I noticed it was time for the first formal assembly. I said goodbye, hung up, and hurried back downstairs.

The only room large enough to hold all eighty students was the sanctuary—another addition to the original estate, but with far more atmosphere than the dining room. Long and narrow, with stained glass windows and a raised platform at the far end, it was far more like a chapel than a lecture hall. I stopped at the entrance and gazed across the rows of chairs. I spotted Janis and Claire near the front at the same time that Janis raised an arm and waved for me to join them.

Unlike the lively energy we'd experienced earlier throughout the building, the atmosphere here demanded quiet reverence. Janet had told us that Stansted had a vibration all its own, built up over the years of students working hand in hand with the spirit world, and I could tangibly feel it from where I sat. When Simon and four tutors walked single file down the center aisle to mark the beginning of the opening session, there was no need to call for silence.

I studied the course leaders as they paraded past, trying to get my first glimpse of Mavis. From her reputation, I knew she had to be older than the rest, but everyone in the group appeared to be in their forties or fifties. I also recalled that there were supposed to be six instructors, but I only counted five.

All but Simon took a seat in chairs on the platform. Now sporting more formal dress slacks and a collared shirt, Simon stepped front and center and welcomed us to the school. He wasted no time in answering the question that must have been on more minds than just mine.

"I understand that some of you may be wondering where Mavis is." He paused, pursed his lips, then said, "I believe she was last sighted at a Little Chef on the M6."

A roar of raucous laughter shattered the sanctuary's veneer of sanctity. I turned in confusion to my friends. Claire leaned in and said, "Little Chefs are the local McDonald's. They're at every exit on the motorway."

I nodded my head. I'd slept through the bus ride from Heathrow and hadn't seen the restaurants Simon joked about, but obviously Mavis liked to eat.

After a few more perfectly timed one-liners, Simon shifted gears and began his formal opening remarks. The more he spoke, the more I could see that he and my mentor Janet were products of the same schooling. They shared a philosophy that had been imparted to them within the very walls where I now sat. Like Janet, Simon had an obvious reverence for his work, and his words set the tone for the week in such a way that those in the room sat spellbound. I had long ago stopped believing that God was a white bearded man sitting in the clouds, but if God had a voice, I'm sure it would sound like Simon James's.

Simon's attitude of respect for the spirit world and for the work of communicating with them was echoed the next morning when I finally met the legendary Mavis Pittilla. I'd half expected to find a larger-than-life woman wearing a shiny tiara. Instead, Mavis looked like an average British grandmother you'd run across in the local butcher shop. A few inches over five feet in height, pleasantly padded, with round cheeks and twinkling eyes, she might as well have been wearing a sign that said, "Hug me."

When she began her lecture on the purpose of mediumship, I fell in love with her voice. Soft and lilting, she spoke with a heavy Manchester accent. Even though her abilities and her long years of experience placed her among the stars of British mediums, I noted not a trace of superiority in her demeanor.

The subject matter of the lecture was nothing new to me. I had written two books on the topic, but that morning Mavis put a medium's work into a whole new light for me. Being a medium was a calling, she said, and I nodded with dawning comprehension. I had been on a mission to prove that the spirit survives death, and that mission had transitioned into something completely unexpected. What else but a calling would cause me to travel so far from my home and so far from my previous line of work?

Then, as if she knew me better than I knew myself, Mavis raised her hand and asked a telling question. "I want to know," she said, nodding at the group to follow her lead and raise their hands, "How many of you could *not* be here right now?"

Her question struck me like a physical blow. It had taken Mavis's question to point out what was now obvious. I had spent the night tossing and turning in a strange, small bed, trying not to awaken my college-age roommates. Rather than greet my husband with a good-morning kiss, I'd whispered my greetings to him through a pay phone in a hallway as others walked by. I was thousands of miles from home in a foreign country, embarking on a personal journey that was even more foreign, yet I couldn't *not* be there. I raised my hand slowly, and as I did so, tears ran unexpectedly down my face.

The situation may have reminded me of my recurring nightmare, but being in Mavis's group was a dream come true. Our group of nine students consisted of seven women and two men, hailing from England, Canada, Denmark, Holland, and Germany. We met for two sessions a day in the estate's library, surrounded by shelves lined with thick leather-bound books about Spiritualism and mediumship.

We arranged our chairs in a small circle that took up only one corner of the large room. Our small number allowed each of us to ask whatever questions came to mind during what felt more like intimate fireside chats than class work. As we learned, we were watched over by the piercing eyes of one of the school's legendary teachers, Gordon Higginson, who peered down at us from a painting hung over the fireplace. He had taught both Mavis and Simon, and from the stories they told of him, he had been a tough taskmaster.

I quickly learned to expect no coddling from Mavis, either, but her style was one of tough love. She pushed us just as hard as Janet, but always with a gentleness that made me want to do well. What struck me most about Mavis's teaching was the obvious love she felt for her work and for the spirit world. Her lessons were laced with pearls of wisdom that kept me scribbling notes every time she spoke.

"Go for the joy of communication from the spirit world. You are here for the people there."

"We can't prove life after death; the spirit world does it."

"First build the belief and faith in your soul's ability. When the conscious mind says, 'I can't do this,' you have negated your soul's ability to give you faith."

I wanted to have faith, but the fear that my experience was not up to the level of the rest of the group seemed well-founded during our initial round of introductions. Mavis asked each of us to describe how we knew that a spirit was present when we were giving a private reading or a public demonstration of mediumship. I listened with envy as each of my classmates described tingling hands, unusual "quickening" feelings, and other physical sensations that I had never experienced. How could I admit that I felt nothing? When my turn came, I simply stated that my desire to feel the spirits' presence was one of my main goals for the course.

Mavis then asked each of us to stand up one by one and give a demonstration of mediumship so she could gauge our abilities. When my turn came to bring through the loved one of someone in the group, I silently thanked Janet for giving me such a strong foundation. As nervous as I was, her system of "name, rank, and serial number," helped me to step onto the raised platform and trust that the spirit world wouldn't let me down.

I may have felt as if I were pulling mere data out of the air that afternoon, but the details perfectly fit the father of one of the two male students from England. I described a man who had died in his sixties from lung problems. I sensed that it was not a recent passing. I felt that he had owned horses and enjoyed painting landscapes. I saw him doing deskwork and writing in a ledger, and I saw an image of a pen that had been special to him.

My classmate, David, confirmed all of the initial evidence, including the fact that his father had been a clerk who always wrote with a favorite fountain pen. I began to feel better, thinking that maybe I wasn't in over my head after all.

When I mentally heard the word "lorry" to describe a large vehicle that flashed through my mind, I knew the thought had come from the spirit world and not from me. I would have used the word "truck."

"That's very good," Mavis said. "Now can you tell us what is *in* the lorry?"

I stared back at her. Was she kidding? It was rare enough for me to see anything clairvoyantly, and when images came, they were as brief as a blink.

Mavis turned to the rest of the group to share a teaching point. "When you see an image in your mind's eye, hold onto it. Don't just let it slip away . . . look further."

She went on to give examples of the kind of detail we could hope to get from these visual pieces of the puzzle: We shouldn't be satisfied with just a truck or what was in the truck, but what was written on the side. Looking further, we should see if it had a recognizable hood ornament. And if we were going to look that closely, she advised us, why not go for a real prize and read the truck's license plate?

I wasn't the only one to let out a dreamy murmur at the thought of bringing through that kind of evidence, but Mavis let us know that when working with the spirit world, anything was possible. Using this method of looking further into visual images, she shared with us how she had brought through actual street names and even four-digit house numbers. In one brief lesson, Mavis Pittilla raised the bar of mediumship to a new level, but one that seemed enticingly within our reach.

"So what's in the lorry?" she asked again, turning back to face me.

I tried to relax and recall the picture. The image of the lorry flashed before my eyes again and I held onto it with my mind. Using nothing more than intention, I looked in the back of the truck and saw vegetables, but was I making this up as I did in my dreams? David had said his father was a clerk. Why would he be driving a truck loaded with produce?

I hesitated to say anything, then remembered Mavis's words about belief and faith.

"It's carrying vegetables."

All eyes turned to David. He nodded and gave me a big thumbs-up. "My father earned most of his money as a clerk, but he worked on his father's farm as well. That lorry would have been full of vegetables from my grandfather's fields."

I might not have felt the presence of spirit as my classmates did, but that day and in the days that followed, I held my own in the practical exercises. I felt far from "advanced," but every session with Mavis brought new insights and methods that I could try out on the spot.

Midway through the week, Mavis proposed an idea that she'd been toying with, but only if the group was game for it. Everyone leaned forward in their chairs and waited to hear her offer. She lowered her voice and asked if we'd like to try some light trance work. The group's enthusiastic reaction was immediate; there was no need to take a vote.

All of us had had practice in readings and demonstrations, but only a few had dabbled in the deeper altered states required for trance. Mavis let us know that working with trance wasn't on the schedule for the week, and that perhaps we shouldn't deviate from the plan. Her words were met with a hailstorm of protests that left no doubt as to our desires.

I had no experience with trance, and could barely contain my excitement at the thought of trying it. I'd read about several famous trance mediums, including a few books about Edgar Cayce, who did all of his work from a deep hypnotic state. Trance work required a high level of trust in the spirit world and a certain level of surrender of one's own will. I was okay with all of that. I didn't believe in the concept of evil spirits, so I had nothing to fear.

Our group returned to the library after lunch to find the lights dimmed. The chairs had been arranged in a semicircle facing a single chair on a small raised platform by the fireplace. We sat and spoke in hushed tones until Mavis entered the room. She sat in one of the chairs near the middle of the semicircle, two seats to my right.

She began the session by stating that she didn't want any of us to go into full trance. We should only enter a light altered state, and we should aim to maintain some awareness. While in this state, Mavis explained, we were to mentally invite someone from the spirit world to blend with our own energy field as completely as possible. We were to relax and let the spirit entity communicate through us in whatever way they desired.

From her description, the light trance state didn't sound any different than what I experienced every day during my meditations, yet the situation felt surreal to me. I was sitting in a darkened room with nine foreigners, waiting to let a bunch of spirit people use our bodies. There was nothing in my life experience to equate with this. I wasn't sure what to expect. Would they speak through us? Would we move around?

I felt a wave of relief when Mavis asked one of the more experienced members of our group to go first. Martin had studied under Mavis for years and seemed perfectly at ease as he settled into the "hot seat" and closed his eyes. Mavis quietly informed the rest of us that we should continue to talk amongst ourselves to help Martin relax.

He didn't seem to need any help. After just a few minutes of deep breathing, his facial features began to twitch.

"Oh, yes," Mavis said softly, "this is very good. Do any of you see anything?"

Beyond the facial movements, I saw nothing, but several of my classmates commented on the changing colors in Martin's aura. Mavis confirmed that she was seeing the same thing, then asked if any of us sensed a change in temperature. If anything, the room felt cooler to me, and several others stated the same thing.

After a few more twitches, Martin opened his mouth and began to speak in a voice quite different from his own.

"Good afternoon," the voice said.

"Good afternoon," Mavis said, "and welcome."

I'm sure my eyes were as big as pie pans. This was beyond fascinating, far better than watching an actor in a sci-fi movie. For a brief moment, the skeptic in me tried to put her two cents in, but I paid her no attention. I didn't know Martin well, but I was a good enough judge of character to know that it was unlikely he was acting.

To my surprise, the voice said nothing more. In retrospect, that makes sense. We were students, after all, not experienced trance mediums. After the initial greeting and two minutes of silence, Mavis thanked the spirit for joining us and invited Martin to return to full consciousness. When he opened his eyes, Mavis congratulated him on doing very well.

Heck, I thought, *if that's all there is to it, I can do that.*

Three more of my classmates followed Martin. Two had no noticeable experience. The third woman, Jenna, seemed to be having some kind of paranormal experience, but the only way I could tell was from the comments of my classmates. My frustration built as Mavis and those around me described the spirit of an older woman who was supposedly overshadowing Jenna's body.

"I wish I could see it," I whispered to Erika, the Dutch girl to my left.

"Relax your eyes completely," she whispered back. "Nearly close your eyelids and let them go out of focus."

As she demonstrated what I was supposed to do, I laughed softly in recognition. Erika had the same dreamy look I'd seen so often on Anne Gehman's face when she tuned in to the spirit world.

I faced Jenna and did as Erika said, relaxing my eyelids and letting my eyes go almost out of focus. The result was immediate, and I gasped. I could clearly see a pair of old ladies' spectacles sitting on Jenna's nose. They were merely a wispy apparition, but they appeared very real.

"She's wearing glasses!" I said, trying my best to keep my voice down.

"That's right," Mavis said softly from my right.

"I see them, too," another student whispered, and described the same rectangular wire-rimmed pair that I saw.

Making a deliberate effort to keep my eyelids and focus relaxed, I noticed that even though Jenna's hair was long and straight, there seemed to be a small, round bun atop her head. Just then, Mavis asked, "Does anyone see the bun on her head?"

Four of us said "yes" in unison. Stunned, I held my droopy eyes riveted on Jenna. The bun and glasses remained, giving my young classmate the appearance of an elderly woman. The scene took me back to Disney World as a child when I'd ridden through the funny house with my parents. Looking in a mirror, we'd seen a ghostly figure riding in the car with us. The same kind of holographic image now seemed to be superimposed over my classmate, but this was no smoke and mirrors mirage. This was the spirit of a woman who had once walked the earth, and who had returned now to help us with our training.

I'm not dreaming. I really see her, and the others see her, too. I suddenly understood how Janet had linked in to the same spirit that I brought through during my first experience with mediumship in her class. She had linked in to the spirit *because he was really there.* It hadn't been impersonal "data" that I pulled from the air, any more than this elderly woman before me was impersonal. I could see her with my two reliable retinas.

This is real, I reminded myself again. *This is reality.* But "reality" had taken on a whole new meaning.

Like a model posing for a group of student artists, Jenna continued to sit before us—perhaps aware of us chatting, perhaps not. No part of her body moved, and no voice came from her throat. She and the old lady simply blended in silence. After several more minutes, the ethereal glasses began to disappear, followed by the bun, which dissolved like a wispy cloud.

"She's going now," Mavis said unnecessarily, for it was plainly clear to me.

Mavis then stood and approached Jenna. "Thank you for coming," she said in a voice like that of a hostess speaking to a guest. "Thank you very much."

Jenna's eyes blinked open, then closed.

"Gently. Gently," Mavis said. "That's it."

When Jenna returned to full consciousness, she walked back to her seat in the semicircle and we all excitedly shared with her what we'd seen. She seemed a bit dazed, and admitted that she hadn't been aware of any presence.

"I feel as if I've just had a good sleep," she said.

"You did an excellent job of allowing," Mavis said to Jenna, then she turned to me and asked, "Would you like to go next?"

Any trepidation I felt was overcome by intense curiosity. I moved the few feet to center stage and sat down on the small chair. Although nervous, I felt safe, for unlike a demonstration of mediumship, I didn't have to produce or prove anything. I simply had to imagine that I was alone at home meditating and try to go a bit deeper than usual. I closed my eyes and shifted around in the chair until I was comfortable.

Unfortunately, my efforts to relax were stymied by the rapid thudding of my heart. *Slow down!* I commanded it, and concentrated on my deep breathing.

I could hear the others talking quietly. Knowing that they weren't staring expectantly at me helped me to not feel so self-conscious. The palpitations subsided, and I began to feel the familiar calm descending. As I went deeper, I remembered Mavis's instructions to mentally invite the presence of any spirit who wanted to work with me. I asked them to step into my aura and blend with me completely. Not knowing what else to do, I began to recite a mental mantra.

I surrender . . . I love you . . . I surrender . . . I love you . . . .

As I repeated the words, I could hear Mavis talking about the beautiful colors in my aura and how my ethereal body was beginning to move back and forth in a shunting motion. This was a new word as well as a new concept for me. I figured I must be doing something right, and slowed my breathing down even more.

I surrender . . . I love you . . . I surrender . . . I love you . . .

I became aware of an unusual fluttery feeling throughout my body—a completely unique physical sensation, unlike anything I'd ever felt. My head felt swirly and I had to fight to keep from tilting to the right. The feeling drifted away, but now I felt pressure against my eyes, as if they were being pressed back in the sockets. I was too fascinated to be frightened.

As much as I wanted to remain relaxed, my pulse quickened when I heard Mavis say, "There's a man and a woman."

She sees two spirits?

What I felt within my body was unique, but I would not have equated it with the presence of spirit. Then again, I had nothing to compare this with. The swirly feeling returned just as Mavis said, "Look, they're switching over."

I felt the pressure in my eye sockets again, just as Mavis said, "It's the man now. Can you all feel the change?"

I knew that by this time all eyes in the room were focused on me just as mine had been on Jenna. I couldn't have cared less how much they stared. All that mattered was riding this weird wave of sensations.

I had been sitting with my feet flat on the floor and my hands resting palm down on my thighs. Suddenly, my right index finger jerked upward and returned to its original position as if it had a mind of its own.

Did that just happen? I wondered. Nobody in the room spoke. I suspected that like me, they were waiting to see what would happen next.

We didn't have to wait long.

Slowly, but without any effort of my own, my right hand raised up ever so slightly, then my hand and arm slid off my lap and hung limply at my side. I willed myself to stay calm.

I surrender . . . I surrender . . . thank you . . . .

My index finger twitched again and a singular thought blazed through my brain: *I did not do that.*

Nor did I consciously do what followed.

Slowly, slowly, as if it weren't attached to my body, my right arm rose a full foot to the side, coming to hover at a forty-five-degree angle from my body. It remained suspended there with no help from me to hold it up. The arm felt as if it were resting on a cushion of air. I felt resistance from beneath it, as if I would have had to exert an effort to push it back down. My shoulder muscles remained completely relaxed and uninvolved.

My mind raced as I realized that my arm was holding itself up. Then I recognized that this was an inaccurate analysis. A *spirit person* was holding it up.

The enormity of the experience suddenly overwhelmed me. Mavis must have felt this, because I could hear her stepping closer as she said, "Slowly . . . slowly . . . relax . . . ."

It was too much. I broke the connection and my arm fell to my side. I slumped forward, put my head in my hands, and burst into tears.

Mavis put her hands on my shaking shoulders.

"I didn't do that," I sobbed. "That wasn't me."

"Of course you didn't, my dear. You did very, very well." She stroked my back and said, "That was as perfect a blending as you could ask for."

Her words only made me cry harder. For the first time since I embarked on this journey, I had no doubt that the spirit world was real. I didn't need the Grande Dame of British mediumship to tell me that a spirit had blended with my own. In answer to yet another prayer, I had felt it for myself.

As I slowly gathered my wits, Mavis asked me to describe what I'd felt. I told her about the repeated swirliness in my head.

"From now on, that's how you'll know that spirit is with you," she said. Then she told me that she felt the male spirit would be working with me in the future—that he was what mediums called a "control."

The thought of having a dedicated helper thrilled me. I felt immense gratitude and love for both of these spirit beings who had made their presence known through me for the sole purpose of helping with my development. More than ever now I wanted to build on that experience and show them that I was as devoted as they were.

With shaking legs I returned to my seat. The next student went to the platform for her turn, but I had a hard time paying attention. I sat in my chair and toyed with my index finger, testing how it felt to move it up and down. I surreptitiously raised my arm a few inches at my side. Each motion took a deliberate, focused effort, requiring the cooperation of mind and muscles. The feeling of exertion was completely different from what I'd experienced on the platform. I was deliberately making these movements. Those on the platform had been done *to* me.

I could no longer deny what my doubt-filled mind had tried so hard to refute. The spirit world was real, and it was filled with intelligent minds capable of making their presence seen, heard, and unmistakably felt. It had taken a monumental effort from those on the other side, but the skeptic in me had finally been squelched. *Thank you, thank you, thank you,* I transmitted to my helpers, along with a huge dose of love.

After the rest of my classmates had their turn on the platform, Mavis admitted that she had hoodwinked us. The real purpose of the exercise, she told us, was to recognize that what we'd done in the light trance state was exactly what happens when giving a reading. The spirit world simply blends with our spirit, she said, just as they had on the platform.

Hoodwinked or not, her methods were brilliant. I now understood how a medium could physically feel what a spirit died of. I understood why a medium's hands might imitate the motions of something the spirit used to do, such as playing a keyboard. I now knew first-hand that with cooperation between the two dimensions, the spirit world could use the medium's physical body to help communicate a myriad of messages.

The next day our group returned to practicing demonstrations of mediumship. When my turn came, I stood somewhat nervously in front of the circle. Unlike the day before, when I'd simply had to sit in the chair and be open, I once again felt the pressure to perform.

"Don't think so much," Mavis advised me. "Just start talking about anything."

"About anything?"

"Yes. Just loosen your tongue and the rest will follow."

"Okay," I shrugged. "I'm standing here in this beautiful library, ready to bring through a spirit that someone here will recognize. I'm really hoping something comes to me soon, because I don't want to stand here all day. "

I felt somewhat foolish for rambling, but as I spoke, I noticed that I felt strangely lightheaded. I swayed a bit, then realized that it wasn't dizziness, but the same swirliness I'd experienced the previous day in the light trance state. My heart surged. It seemed that everything I learned in class was turned into experience at the next opportunity, building up a stable foundation to which I could always return.

"I'm feeling the presence of spirit now," I said, as a series of mental sensations filled my mind.

With my tongue loosened, I proceeded to share aloud what I was seeing, sensing, and hearing.

"I see flowers," I said, "fresh flowers in vases. There are vases all around an elegant house, and this feels very British, so this is someone who lived in England. I see a woman sitting in front of a fireplace reading. She has a blanket over her lap. She's older, but not too elderly. This woman loves to read. I see books on shelves on both sides of a fireplace. Can anyone take any of this?"

Mavis nodded. "Yes. You have my aunt."

I smiled. I'd remarked earlier that more of Mavis's family members came through in class than anyone else's. She told us it was because her loved ones in spirit were used to helping her out.

"Okay," I said, "I get the sense that this woman liked to listen to Bach and Beethoven."

"Absolutely," Mavis confirmed.

"She was very much into the arts and she was very reserved and quiet."

"That's correct."

"I sense that she didn't like to cook."

"Yes."

"And I sense that this woman was sickly all of her life. She was very susceptible to colds and the flu. She eventually died from congestion in the lungs. I sense that she either couldn't walk or had difficulty walking."

"I can accept all of that. She broke her hip at the end, and eventually died of pneumonia."

I was amazed at the number of details and the clarity of the attunement. The difference in just a few days of classes was like changing a radio from a scratchy AM station to a clear FM signal.

"I don't sense any children around her," I continued, "and I feel that she was married, but there's no husband around."

"Yes, that's very good. She did marry, but he left her after only four days."

The class murmured their surprise.

I waited for more, but nothing came to me. "That's all I'm sensing," I said.

"Yes, you dropped the link," Mavis said, "but I would be very pleased with that contact."

I certainly was. Still, I felt I could have done better. I recalled that earlier in the week Mavis had taught us to take the time after every reading or demonstration to ask the spirit world how we could have done better. I decided to use the meditation period that followed the class to do so.

Our small group went immediately from the practice session to the sanctuary, where we joined the other students. As Simon led us with guided imagery into a light altered state, I invited Mavis's aunt to blend with me. I didn't feel her presence as I had earlier, but trusting that she was still around, I asked her to show me if I could have brought her through any differently.

Suddenly, just like the day before, my right finger jumped, startling me.

By this time, Simon had stopped talking to allow us time to sit quietly. I knew I had at least twenty minutes of uninterrupted silence. I decided to go with the flow and simply allow.

At first, nothing else happened, then I became aware of my hand rising from my lap. Once again, I did a mental check. I was definitely not moving it myself, but now the hand floated in a wavelike motion from left to right. Deliberately holding the link, I opened my eyes and looked down to make sure I wasn't imagining the whole experience. Sure enough, my hand was gently rocking back and forth. With instant recognition, I knew what was going on.

My hand was petting a cat.

Was this possible? Had Mavis's aunt owned a cat, I wondered? Was this what she was showing me with this visible, tangible sign?

My hand lowered into my lap, and I thanked the spirit for her help. As soon as the meditation ended, I made a beeline for the dining room. It was lunchtime, and I hoped I might find Mavis there. Sure enough, I spied her on the far side of the room at the tutors' table. Feeling like a school kid entering the teachers' inner sanctum, I knelt at Mavis's side.

"I'm sorry to bother you," I said.

"Not at all," she smiled, and set down her fork.

Lowering my voice to avoid being heard by the other tutors, I described what I'd experienced in the sanctuary. "Am I crazy for thinking I was petting a cat?" I asked.

Mavis gave me a big smile. "Absolutely not! She did have a cat, and that's exactly what she would have done."

I thanked her and joined Janis and Claire at their table. I barely tasted my food as I shared the latest happenings.

"That's so cool!" Janis said.

"Good stuff," said Claire.

How I loved these women! I would have hesitated to share my stories with anyone else at that point, but my friends made me feel as if nothing I could say would shock them. Having a spirit woman move my hand to pet her cat was just one more exciting phase in the development of a medium's abilities. I asked about their own experiences, and their stories let me know that there was no limit to the things the spirit world could teach us. We were all having an awesome week.

The days were long, full, and exciting, but exhausting. The large group lectures continued to inform and inspire. The meditations brought new insights, but nothing compared with the intimacy of the small group work. For our final lesson, Mavis tasked us to give two back-to-back private readings with our fellow students. In spite of being together in the classroom all week, we still knew very little about each other. This was deliberate. Mavis had asked us at the beginning of the week not to interact with each other outside of the classroom. Now we approached this final graduation exercise with a clean slate.

I was paired up with my British classmate, Martin. With only ten minutes per reading, I got straight down to business. Because this was an exercise, I went through the motions of introducing myself and giving an introduction to mediumship as if it were an actual reading. Martin smiled tolerantly and pretended to hear the information for the first time.

I then took a few breaths and invited a spirit who had known Martin to blend with my energy. Within seconds I felt the swirliness. Relieved and excited, I waited, then a white cross flashed through my mind. It didn't look like the crosses in most Christian churches, so I described it to Martin as I saw it—thick and square, with the horizontal cross bar exactly in the middle. Remembering Mavis's teaching, I held onto the image and looked further. Sure enough, the vision expanded.

"I see the cross standing on a small dark table with a red cloth on it. I'm aware of a man in a long, white robe that comes all the way to the floor. I see a gold sash down the front with lots of embroidery. This is obviously a priest, but I don't know what this combination of colors means. Does any of this make sense to you?"

"Yes, it does," Martin said.

"Okay. I'm getting images of the little white hosts a priest uses, but I'm also sensing loaves of bread for some reason. This is a tall man, and he's very solidly built. I get the sense of him standing with his arms spread open in welcome and a big smile on his face."

"Okay, that's very good," Martin said. "I know who you have. He was a priest, and he liked to bake bread. Go on."

I was amazed. Janet had said the energy at Stansted was special, but with the clarity of the images and the amount of detail I was getting, someone seemed to have turned up the power to a whole new level.

"Now I see a long, white building with lots of windows across the front, like a dormitory. Next to it is another building, and the word "abbey" just popped into my mind. It has a tall bell tower. Unlike the white building, this one is made of bricks. It has big, double doors at the front."

"I know the place you're describing."

I shook my head in disbelief, but continued. "I'm hearing this priest say, 'It's glorious in the afterlife. You're going to love it here.' Does any of this make sense?"

"Yes, it does. Can you tell me what he has in his hand?"

"What?" I hadn't expected to be asked a question.

"What's he holding in his hand?"

I exhaled loudly. Questions brought the active mind into play. Stay receptive. Stay passive.

I looked . . . and saw a necklace.

"I see two strands of a necklace lying across an outstretched palm."

"Perfect," Martin said. "The man you're describing was an Anglo-Catholic priest I was friends with. The unusual cross is the Celtic cross. He would be holding a rosary, which would look like a necklace if he were holding it. He used to wear a robe and embroidered gold sash exactly as you described it. You also described perfectly the abbey where he worked, and next to it was a school, which would have been the long, white building with lots of windows. I knew this man in life, but he is now one of my spirit guides. He comes to me often to talk about the other side."

A spirit guide? I had shied away from people's talk about guides, because there never seemed to be any proof. This guide had given me plenty of proof.

"Your time is up," Mavis announced. "Those of you who just received a reading, please move one seat to your right."

I waited as half of the group shifted chairs. My brain and body buzzed with excitement and nerves. *So far so good.*

My classmate David came to take Martin's place. I greeted him and quickly went through the introductory remarks. When I began the actual reading, the first thing I saw was a tall, brown horse.

"Okay, this horse has a saddle," I said, stunned at how quickly I'd gotten the image, especially on the tail of the previous reading. "And there's a young man standing facing the horse, holding the reins. He's tall and thin. Now I see a young girl standing to the side of the horse."

I stared into space, fascinated. It was like watching a picture being painted as new images superimposed themselves upon the original image of the horse. I described it to David as it unfolded in my mind.

"The young girl reminds me of Alice in Wonderland. She's younger than the boy, with long, wavy blond hair and a skirt that comes to her knees with pleats all around it. Does any of this make sense?"

"Yes, it does. Go on."

"The boy is feeding the horse some hay. I don't think either of these people with the horse is in the spirit world . . . but now I'm aware of a man," I said, as I felt the swirliness for the first time. "It's as if he's watching this scene with me. He's reaching out now and stroking the girl's hair. He has a grandfatherly feel, but it may not be the grandfather. Can you understand that?"

"Yes," David said, smiling now, "That's very good. You're describing my children when they were younger, and that was the horse they used to take care of. The one watching them would be my brother, who was much older and was like a grandfather to them. He's the one in spirit."

I shook my head. "Okay, well now he's showing me a daisy. This either has something to do with the actual flower, or—" an interesting thought popped into my mind. "—or he wants to talk about somebody named Daisy. Do you know a Daisy?"

"Yes, I do."

"You do?" Goose bumps broke out on my arms and legs. Then I started nodding. "Yes . . . yes . . . He's letting me know that Daisy hasn't been well, but that she's going to be okay."

"That's right," David said, smiling. "Daisy is my children's godmother, and she hasn't been well, but she seems to be getting better."

"Holy mackerel." I took a deep breath. I was enjoying the exercise, but it was stressful holding the link. I glanced up at Mavis as she walked by, and she motioned for me to keep going.

"Okay, now I'm seeing this man—your brother—in a pub. I see him leaning on the bar as if he's really comfortable in this place."

David laughed. "That would be my brother."

Incredulous, I described the full-screen images that ran through my head. "He's surrounded by his buddies. He's tilting back a big pint of beer, as if to show me that he really enjoyed a pint or two . . . and he smoked. In fact, that's how he died—from a problem with his lungs from smoking, isn't it?"

"Yes, it is."

"Wow. Okay. I get the sense that unlike your father, who was a clerk, this man was a laborer. He worked with his hands. They're really big hands, and they're rough."

"Yes," David said. "He was a machinist."

Now I started to sense personality along with the visual images. "I feel that he had a great sense of humor. In fact, he was quite the jokester. He had a hearty laugh, too—a real 'har, har, har' kind, and I have this image of him slapping you really hard on the back."

"That's exactly what he'd do."

My time was almost up. I couldn't have been happier with the details, but I knew this was my final hurrah. Janet No-havec taught that a medium should always 'go for wow.' The things I'd given David so far were spot on, but I wanted one more really big 'wow.' *What would Mavis do?* I wondered, and once again I recalled her advice: *Look further.*

When I'd brought through David's father at the beginning of the week, I saw the lorry. I'd looked further and seen the produce in the back, but that was as far as I'd gone. I didn't hold on long enough to get a make or model. I didn't get a license plate. I didn't believe I could. The week at Stansted had been all about faith and belief—about pushing our abilities to the limit. It was about stretching ourselves as far as we could go.

It was time for one final stretch.

I closed my eyes and brought back the image of David's brother in the pub. *Okay, buddy, help me out here.* I looked around the pub. He was still leaning on the bar, but I could see the carpet now, and it was red. The paneling was dark. I described the scene to David, and he nodded his head.

Not good enough . . . not good enough . . . most pubs have dark paneling and red carpet.

I looked further, and then I saw it—a wooden sign hanging out front. It was rectangular, with round scallops at each corner. In the center of the sign was an elaborate coat of arms in red and black, and across the top of the sign were bold, black letters. I caught my breath, for I could clearly read the words.

Could it be? There was only one way to find out. I felt like a game show contestant going for the final prize as I said, "The name of the pub where your brother hung out was The King's Arms."

David knew how much that piece of evidence meant to me. It was the golden egg. He beamed back at me and nodded. "That's right."

"That's it? That was the name of the pub where he drank?"

"That's right," he repeated. "The King's Arms."

I raised my eyes to the heavens and squeezed them tight. No "A" in school had ever felt so good. Even Janet would agree, "The King's Arms" was a "wow." The lines of communication with the spirit world were wide open.

That evening, the full complement of students and tutors gathered in the sanctuary for the final assembly with Simon. His booming voice resounded through the hall as he recapped with his usual eloquence just how special the week had been. Yes, it was special for the camaraderie we'd shared, and for the new things we had learned. It was special for the communion we'd enjoyed with the spirit world, but it was special for yet another reason. This week, he reminded us, we had celebrated the anniversary of the birthday of Spiritualism.

I pulled a tissue from my bag and dabbed at my eyes. I hadn't always been so emotional, but there truly was something unique about the energy at Stansted. I had cried at the beginning of the week, but my tears flowed now for a different reason. Janet's prediction was right—attending the school was a life-changing experience. I was a different person than the one who'd lugged her bags down the hall seven days earlier.

Now, as I listened to Simon's farewells, I thanked God for the transformation that had taken place within me. I had come to this school to learn to trust those in the spirit world, to feel their presence and to deepen my connection with them. I had accomplished all of these goals, and I now knew beyond any doubt that their world was very real. I had seen them with my physical eyes. I had heard them. I had tangibly felt them, and I had formed a partnership with them that I was now determined to uphold.

Exactly 151 years before, the movement to communicate with the spirit world was officially born. As we celebrated that day in the sanctuary of Stansted Hall, I realized it wasn't just the birthday of Spiritualism—it was my birthday, too—my birthday as a medium.

How do you seize a moment?
How do you hold it in your hand?
You stop the frantic motion
And freeze right where you stand.

It takes a dedication
From a moment of decision
To let Spirit guide your life –
To your old habits make revision.

"I seize this day as mine," you say,
"A day to see things as they are –
Not the way I have been told
By those who saw things from afar."

"Instead, I will be guided
By One who sees truly without eyes –
By the one true guiding force
That lights up all the skies."

"And when I lose my way,
On this Force I will now call.
For with God to light the way,
There's no way that I can fall."

Seize the day—seize every moment
To with God your soul unite,
And leave behind the darkness
As Spirit leads you to the light.

9

Going for "Wow!"

My prayers were answered at Arthur Findlay College,
but I hadn't anticipated the adjustment those answers would
require. I had several noteworthy experiences at the school,
but once I got back to my regular life, I found it difficult to
share those experiences with friends and family. I genuinely
feared the reaction I'd get if I told people that a spirit person
had levitated my arm. I couldn't blame anyone for thinking I
might have left a few of my marbles back in England.

Still, I knew what I had experienced. The sense of certainty that the spirit world was real didn't fade with time. In fact,
as I read and re-read my notes from the college, my conviction that I had interacted mentally and physically with intelligent minds on the other side only grew stronger. In quiet
moments alone, I tried out my new identity.

I am a medium.

The words felt strange on my tongue. I tested them again.
"I am a medium."

My insides clenched when I thought of saying the words
to someone else. My problem was a basic human weakness:
I didn't want to be different. I didn't want to be thought of as
"weird."

Then why did you study mediumship, the voice inside my
head chided.

And as always, that voice of reason brought me instantly
back to reality. I could never forget why I had decided to

study mediumship. Every time I passed Susan's picture in
our home, every time someone mistakenly called me "Susan"
instead of "Suzanne," every time I saw my husband drift off to
that melancholy place that he kept to himself, I remembered
why I had made that decision.

"I am a medium," I said aloud, and it felt okay.

I had turned off Main Street onto a very narrow side road
that many would never dare to venture down. That road
would doubtless have its bumps, but I could handle it. I could
not deny what I had experienced and demonstrated in England. Those events were part of the "new me." I no longer
believed that the spirit world was real, I *knew* it was. My concept of reality had changed over a very short period of time; I
merely had to adjust to it.

Part of that adjustment would mean dealing with skeptics,
but I wouldn't fall into the trap of arguing. Being a skeptic
myself, I understood that only personal experience could
shift a person from doubt to certainty. It was my task to give
people details about their loved ones that I couldn't possibly
know. What they chose to think about that evidence was up
to them.

Flush with success from my final two readings at Stansted,
I was anxious to see if I could produce the same level of detail
in private readings at home. Family members wouldn't do,
because I knew too much about their loved ones on the other
side. Friends were the obvious choice, but we had only recently moved to Florida. I wasn't sure how open-minded my
new neighbors would be to my unusual vocation.

Jan Blythe, a transplant from New England, lived kitty-
corner across the street from me. When Ty and I first moved
in, I felt inexplicably drawn to Jan, but we never seemed to
connect. I would pass by her house and feel unusually frustrated that we hadn't yet gotten to know each other. I couldn't

shake the feeling that we were somehow *supposed* to be
friends. About ten years older than I, she had an easy, laid-
back disposition and a warm smile that gave her a sisterly feel.

Just before I left for England, Jan and I happened to be
in our front yards at the same time. I mentioned that I was
going overseas, and when Jan heard the reason, she showed a
genuine curiosity. She enthusiastically told me how she and
her sister, Carolyn, had visited the nearby Spiritualist community in Cassadaga, Florida. When I told her that I'd written
a book about a medium who used to live and work in Cassadaga, we found our common link.

Jan showed up at my front door shortly after my return
from Stansted. She wanted to hear about my experiences at
the college. As I shared some of the details, I clearly heard
the suggestion, *Give her a reading*, and felt a little shiver. She
seemed like the perfect test case, but if I did poorly, I would
have to face her for years to come. Then I reminded myself
that the spirit world had no intention of letting me down.

Jan was more than willing to be my guinea pig, but as I sat
across from her, I found it difficult to quiet my mind. Things
had been a bit hectic since my return, and my thoughts
bounced back and forth like a ping-pong ball. To add to the
difficulty, the fast-paced music I'd been listening to while
jogging a short time earlier continued to bang out a jarring
rhythm in my brain. I concentrated on my breaths and sent
out my desire to make the best connection possible.

I surrender. Please blend with me, I beseeched Jan's relatives in the spirit world.

And finally, I sensed them—a man and a woman who felt
a bit more distant than immediate family members. Right
away the man showed me a red sports car, and I sensed that
he was a bit of a risk-taker. Jan confirmed that she had an
uncle on the other side who had driven a red sports car and

was known for being a daredevil. That was all the confirmation I needed to keep going.

I saw the spirit woman kissing a cross and I got a very strong Catholic feeling. "I sense that the church was this woman's life," I told Jan after passing along the other impressions. "She didn't just go to church on Sunday; it was really important to her."

Jan nodded and told me this sounded very much like her Aunt Lucy.

Next I saw a large gray stone church. Jan confirmed that most Catholic churches were red brick and most protestant churches were gray stone, but her aunt had attended a gray stone Catholic church.

I described the woman as reserved and not very affectionate. I saw her using a cane later in life. The name Francis fluttered through my mind. I rarely heard or sensed names, so I held my breath while waiting for Jan's feedback.

Her face lit up. "Lucy raised my father, who goes by Frank, but his real name is Francis!"

"Wow!" I said. "This is incredible. I can't believe all the visual images I'm getting."

"What else do you see?"

I waited quietly, knowing I had to remain passive and receptive. The time between details seemed far too long for me, but Jan didn't seem to mind. Impatient, I asked Lucy to put something in my hand that would mean something to Jan. Rather than seeing something in response to my request, I heard the word "chocolate."

"Wow," Jan said at this detail. "Aunt Lucy had a real sweet tooth. She never left the house without a candy bar in her pocket." Jan went on to confirm the earlier evidence, telling me that Lucy had worked in an office and she walked with a cane in later life.

"As for your uncle," I said, "he just showed me a pair of boxing gloves. Do you know if he boxed?"

"I don't remember that."

I winced. *Was that strike one?*

Now I rubbed my left leg with both hands and said, "I get the feeling he walked with a limp."

Jan shook her head. "It could be. I just don't know. We weren't that close."

Strike two? I tried not to let my doubts drag down my energy. It was critical to keep my personal vibration as high as possible to hold the link with the spirit world's very high frequency.

Once again the man showed me a red car. I got the feeling he was very proud of that car. He drove fast and lived hard, I told Jan. I described him as solidly built, balding, and under age 60 when he passed. These things Jan could confirm. As for the others, she'd have to check.

The next day, Ty told me how Jan had come running across the street and talked with him while he was working in the yard.

"Tell Suzanne I checked with my aunt. My Uncle Victor liked to box and he walked with a limp!"

I let out a victory whoop. Rather than two strikes, I'd hit a home run. Since Jan hadn't known those evidential details about her uncle, that meant I hadn't been merely reading her mind during the reading. The information had to have come straight from the source.

Thank you, Uncle Victor!

As Ty and I prepared to head to our boat for a summer of sailing, I fit in four more readings. This time I chose fellow students from a Reiki class I'd attended several months earlier. Three of the four sessions produced the same level of detail as Jan's reading. I felt I was on a roll until the fifth reading. Suddenly, it was as if I'd hit a wall. The woman sat across from me and denied knowledge of almost everything and everyone I brought through.

As much as I tried to bolster my confidence, I felt my energy taking a nose-dive.

I soldiered on, telling the woman the words I heard and the feelings I sensed. She stared back at me with a frown.

"Is any of this making sense to you?" I asked, trying to keep the frustration from my voice.

"Well . . . " she wrinkled her nose. "Maybe . . . ."

I sighed. I didn't want "maybe." I wanted an unmistakable "wow."

After half an hour of painful rejection, I finally gave up. "I don't know what's going on," I said to the woman, "but this is just not working."

"Maybe it's me," she said. "I've been told I'm hard to read for."

That might have been true, but I took it personally. Immediately after she left the house I called my mentor.

"Janet," I moaned, "I just gave a reading and totally bombed."

"Welcome to the world of mediumship," she said. "How many readings have you given now, anyway?

I sighed. "Five."

Her laugh seemed a bit too raucous for me, but I couldn't help but give a little chuckle of my own.

"You've given five readings and you're worried about one of them being bad?" she said. "You'd better get used to it, Suzanne. This is not a perfect science."

Janet reminded me that our work was all about attuning with very specific frequencies, and she went over the possible reasons things hadn't gone well. It could have been a vibrational interference the sitter was putting out with her thoughts. It could have been that my energy was low to begin with. It could have been the alignment of the stars, for all we knew. Whatever the cause, she encouraged me not to lose hope and to get right back in the saddle.

That evening, Ty and I entertained a couple of new friends in our home. Ty had met them on the golf course and thought that I would like them. He was right. We chatted comfortably as we sipped wine and munched on hors d'oeuvres. The conversation consisted of the normal getting-to-know-you questions about family and places we'd lived. The woman shared that she'd been one of four children growing up, but it was now just her and her older sister, because her two brothers had died.

"My gosh," I said, noting that our guests were no older than we, "they died pretty young, huh?"

She lowered her eyes. "Yeah."

Without thinking, I blurted out, "Cancer for one and heart for the other."

The woman looked at me as if I'd spoken in Swahili. She turned to her husband and said, "Did you hear what she said? *'Cancer for one and heart for the other!'*" She looked back at me and said, "That's right!"

The unspoken, *How did you know that?* hung between us.

By this time I'd learned to sense when it was appropriate to talk about my new abilities and when to keep them to myself. Somehow I knew that a discussion of mediumship was better left for another time. I smiled back at her, gave a little shrug, and changed the conversation.

Inside, however, I was thrilled. I hadn't been trying to attune to her energy or to that of her brothers, but the information was instantly there. It could have been a case of telepathy rather than the actual presence of her brothers' spirits, but whatever the source, I had successfully tapped into some unseen vibrations. The experience took the edge off the sting of the failed reading earlier in the day.

After our company left and we cleared the dishes, Ty and I decided to get some fresh air. We snapped on Rudy and Gretchen's leads, popped them in the car, and headed for the boardwalk by our local lake.

"Come here," Ty said when we got to the water's edge. "I want to show you something I noticed yesterday."

He led me to the boardwalk's railing and pointed down. "Look at that."

My eyes widened with delight. Through the murky water I could see several circular depressions in the sand. They were about three feet in diameter, and one large carp hovered exactly in the center of each circle.

"Cool!" I exclaimed. "They're like underwater nests to lay their eggs in."

We walked slowly along the railing, silently studying the circles, then returned to our walk. A few yards farther on, we nodded in greeting to a couple sitting on one of the waterside benches. They appeared to be in their early seventies. The woman was tall, with straight, dark brown hair, and she had a runner's lean build. The man was a bit more filled out with a full head of wavy hair. Both returned our greeting with warm smiles of their own.

"Nice camera," Ty remarked to the man.

He seemed pleased with the compliment.

Ty asked a question about the lens, and the two launched into an animated discussion about photography.

I sidled up to the woman and said, "Want to see some-thing really neat?"

She looked surprised, then smiled and said, "Sure."

I motioned for her to follow me and led her to the water's edge. "The fish have made circles in the sand to lay their eggs. Look."

She peered down, then exclaimed with the same sense of wonder I'd felt when I first saw them.

I shook my head and said, "Nature is so awesome."

"It is," she said softly. "It truly is."

She looked up at me and we shared a smile. As we did so, a silent recognition of something beyond ourselves—yet part of both of us—passed between us.

We rejoined the men and their conversation. I learned that the two took photos of the local area every evening and posted them on a blog that was viewed by people all over the world. They then took a picture of Ty and me holding Rudy and Gretchen for their site. Before we departed, Lowell and Lois Anne Anderson formally introduced themselves, and we exchanged cards.

The next morning marked our last day at home for the next six months. As I bustled about packing supplies for the boat, I couldn't shake the feeling that I had met Lois Anne for a reason. *I'm supposed to give her a reading*, I thought. With our trip looming so close, the timing wasn't the greatest, but I had no idea when I'd get to give my next reading. If I was going to get back in the saddle and regain my confidence, this might be my last chance for a while.

I went in search of Ty and found him sorting through paperwork in the study. "I want to see if Lois Anne from last night would like a reading."

Ty had been exceedingly tolerant of my new activities, but now he couldn't hide his surprise. "We're leaving tomorrow!"

"I know," I said. "She'd have to come today, and if she can't make it, then it's not meant to be."

He gave me a resigned shrug and said, "Whatever you want."

I pulled out the business card that Lowell and Lois Anne gave us the night before. The address showed that they lived a good 45 minutes away. I hoped this wouldn't matter to Lois Anne, and dialed the number. I tried putting myself in her place as the phone rang. I could clearly imagine how unusual my offer for a reading might seem to her. After all, I hadn't mentioned the fact that I was a baby medium when we met.

If Lois Anne seemed surprised, it was only that I had called her at all. More than anything, she sounded excited at the prospect of a reading. When I explained that we were leaving the next day and that she would have to come within the next few hours, she wasn't the slightest bit deterred. She agreed to come over right away.

Happily, I not only got back in the saddle, but I had a pretty good ride. I brought through Lois Anne's maternal grandmother and her father with enough evidence to paint a clear picture of both of them. While I would have liked to get more exotic details, Lois Anne was quite excited when I mentioned the vanilla candles her grandmother used to keep around the house and a clock of hers that held great meaning to her family. She connected the image of Abraham Lincoln that I saw to her father's large collection of Lincoln pennies.

My throat constricted with emotion when her father sent me a personal message of reassurance about my work. I clearly heard him saying, "You have to trust this. You're doing fine. Tell her I'm really here and that we're around all the time." I passed this on to Lois Anne, and she reached for the tissues I'd placed beside her chair.

In spite of the "hits" with her father and grandmother, I failed to connect with Lois Anne's mother. She had mentioned to me before the reading that she'd lost her mother not too many years back, but try as I might, I couldn't sense a maternal presence. I emphasized to Lois Anne that this in no way indicated a lack of desire or effort on her mother's part. As always, it was simply a matter of not being able to match our frequencies. I promised that we'd try again when I returned from our sailing trip.

Finding people to give readings to while traveling by sailboat proved to be as difficult as I'd imagined it would be. After two months of cruising the New England coast, I'd only found 3 opportunities to give individual readings. They'd gone well, but I worried that I'd lose what progress I'd made.

Janet Nohavec had advised me to keep pen and paper nearby when I meditated. She had the strong sense that I would be doing automatic writing—receiving messages from the other side while in a light altered state. I could see how this would help me to keep my mediumistic skills sharp. It required the same kind of passive focus to listen for messages from the other side whether I had a client or not.

Over a period of several weeks I did, in fact, hear and write down a few phrases that passed through my mind in meditation. The words were beautiful and philosophical in nature, but each time I chalked the experience up to a vivid imagination.

Then, one very ordinary morning at anchor, I had a meditative experience that was far from ordinary. I sat in my usual chair in the aft cabin with my eyes closed. My finger twitched unexpectedly, and with the twitch came the urge to pick up the nearby pen and paper. I clearly heard several phrases and wrote them down as they came to me. It took about four lines of writing before I noticed there was something different about these words from others I'd gotten in the past.

The words were rhyming.

The realization hit me with a physical jolt as I recognized the brilliance of those in the spirit world. They had figured out that I would never believe I wasn't making up their words unless they gave them to me in a form of writing that I had always shied away from: poetry.

As I held the link, line after line flowed from my mind to the paper. I turned three pages with my eyes closed before the words stopped. Because of the light trance state, I wasn't consciously aware of the content of what I'd written—only that I had produced something cohesive and meaningful. This realization shook me to the core and left me sobbing into my hands when the words finally stopped.

When I emerged from the aft cabin, Ty asked me what was wrong. It was impossible to keep anything secret on a 46-foot boat, and he had heard me crying.

I shook my head. "Something happened. I think I wrote a poem, but it didn't come from me." He seemed rightfully confused. "You think you wrote a poem?"

I explained about the rhyming phrases that had flowed nonstop. If, as I suspected, the three pages of slanted script in my hand resulted in a full-fledged poem, the spirit world had gone overboard to prove themselves to me.

My suspicions proved correct. By the time I finished reading the meaningful verses aloud, both of us were in tears. Ty knew that I had only been in the aft cabin for a few minutes. He also knew that I had never been one to read or write poetry. The pages in my notebook represented nothing less than a blaring sign from the spirit world that I was not alone on my new path as a medium.

When the rhyming messages continued beyond the first week and the pages began to pile up, I recognized another benefit to the poems. Just as I suspected when Janet suggested I try automatic writing, receiving the poetry required the same skills that I used in an actual reading. I could only hear the rhyming words if I sat quietly and remained passively receptive. The moment I let my active mind try to take part in the wording or the theme of the poetry, the words stopped. It no longer mattered if I couldn't find anyone with whom to practice. I was now connecting with the spirit world on a daily basis.

The first few poems applied specifically to me and my personal development. As the days went on, I noticed that the words had taken on more universal themes. I shared the first few by email with a handful of friends who I felt would appreciate that the poems were coming from the spirit world. We all seemed to enjoy the daily exchange of comments and the spiritual discussions the poetry engendered.

After receiving nearly two dozen poems, I received an email from my neighbor, Jan. "Do you think the poets could answer personal questions from other people?"

Her question took me aback. It had never occurred to me to ask them a personal question, let alone someone else's. Once I considered the possibility, it made perfect sense that they would answer. I had no doubt that the poems were coming from a source of intelligence and wisdom outside myself. The poetry was simply a unique form of mediumship. Why wouldn't they have access to information that I couldn't possibly know?

"I don't see why not," I replied. "Send me a question when you come up with one."

Jan wasted no time getting back to me. Her email arrived mid-afternoon, and I told Ty that I was going to the aft cabin to do a special meditation. I sat in my chair and closed my eyes. As I entered the familiar light altered state, I invited the poets to blend with my energy. I felt no swirliness, but trusted they were with me.

What is Jan supposed to do with the information she is learning from your poetry? I asked silently. *Please tell her what her role is in all of this.*

I was as curious as Jan to see how the poets would respond. I sat patiently with the pad of paper and pen in my lap. When my right finger jerked upward, I picked up the pen and waited. The words soon followed . . . .

> *Your role, your role*
> *Has to do with the soul.*
> *Clear the slate.*
> *Clean the plate.*
> *Use these words before it's too late.*

The poets went on in their unique way to say that Jan would continue to find comfort in the poems and that she would carry their messages forward to others who needed her help . . . .

> *You know who this is*
> *Without our saying.*
> *You've been praying*
> *For a way to help them heal.*
> *This inside you feel.*
> *It's real, this urge*
> *Like a wave it does surge.*

On and on they went. As usual, when the poets stopped, I only had a vague idea of what I'd written. I laid down the pen and reviewed the words. The poetry wasn't especially well structured, but it carried a clear message. I had planned to type it and send it to Jan later, but I was anxious for feedback faster than I could get by email. I went on deck and dialed her number. We were anchored off an island along the coast of Maine. Cell phone service was usually poor, so I smiled when her phone started to ring.

"Jan. I got an answer for you!" I said when she picked up.

"Really? Can you read it to me?"

"Of course."

I read slowly, unsure how the words would strike her. Was it true that she had an urge to help others, as the poets said? Had she, indeed, been praying about this?

"Wow," she said softly when I finished. "That really speaks to me."

"You're not just saying that?"

"No," she insisted. "There's a big issue going on with my family, and I've been feeling a lot lately that I'm supposed to help in some way. What do you think they meant by 'Clear the slate,' and 'Use these words before it's too late?'"

"I don't know," I said. "Sounds a little ominous, doesn't it?"

"Yeah," she laughed nervously. "Do you think you could ask them to explain?"

I laughed, too, wondering how far this would go. "Why not? But let's wait until tomorrow." I didn't want to get carried away and spend all my time in meditation.

The next morning the Council of Poets dictated their daily poem. When I sensed the end of the final stanza, I asked Jan's question: *Would you tell us what you meant yesterday by 'Clear the slate before it's too late?'*

The poets wasted no time explaining themselves directly to Jan:

> *You've distant memories stored away.*
> *Bring them forward, this we say.*
> *Hide them not for they do damage.*
> *If it hurts, don't worry—you will manage*
> *To clean the windows, so to speak,*
> *Of your soul—just take a peek.*

"Clear the slate" means wipe it clean
So these your memories will be seen.
Freedom comes when you can close your eyes
And see then with great surprise
That there's nothing more to frighten you
But, in fact, enlighten you.

When I read the poem to Jan later on the phone, she was quiet for a moment, then she let out a long whistle. "Every time I close my eyes to meditate," she admitted, "I get this overwhelming sense of panic."

"Wow," I said, and reread the line, 'Freedom comes when you can close your eyes.'"

"I guess I have some work to do," she said with a tight laugh.

"Sounds that way," I replied.

I agreed to ask if the poets had any further advice the next time I meditated. In fact, they had plenty to say. Over the next three days they dictated three poems revealing a private matter that seemed almost too personal for me to broach. If what the poems said was true, it was no wonder Jan had trouble sitting alone in the silence.

"That's what I thought this was all about," she said, when I read her the disturbing details.

I was stunned. Not only had the poets been correct about Jan's harboring old hurts, but they hit the nail on the head about the cause of those hurts.

The spirits seemed to know that Jan needed a bit of encouragement, for they concluded with some reassuring words for her:

Worry not.
A loving husband have you got.
You lie protected in your bed.
Rest each night your weary head
And know that sleep will come now
When day is done now.
Nothing can any longer hurt you
As we said, we won't desert you.

Rather than being disturbed by the content of the poems, Jan seemed genuinely buoyed by this loving support from the spirit world. She expressed her gratitude to me and to the unseen helpers that were so clearly aware of her troubles.

Her unquestioning acceptance and appreciation fueled my desire to find out how much more we could learn from the poets. The potential seemed limitless. I felt as if I'd found a genie in a bottle. Still, so far I had tested the question-and-answer system with only one person. Ever the skeptic, I needed more than just Jan to increase my trust that the answers weren't coming from me.

I immediately thought of Lois Anne. Our chance encounter had resulted in a valued friendship between kindred spirits, and we regularly shared our ideas and insights with each other via email. Once I began posting the poems each morning in a blog, Lois Anne commented on every one. A retired English teacher, she never found fault with them. When the critic in me spoke up, she kept me going with her positive feedback.

I sent Lois Anne an email and told her how Jan and I had been asking questions and getting answers from the Council of Poets. She responded with great enthusiasm, eager to participate in our experiment with the spirit world.

"I have many questions," she wrote, "but one stands out above all the rest: Should I have done anything to keep my mom alive longer?"

My eyes grew wide as I read the words. This was heavy-duty stuff I was dealing with. The "genie in bottle" was a fun analogy, but Lois Anne's question instantly sobered me. I knew that her mother had died of colon cancer, but I had no knowledge of any of the circumstances surrounding her passing. Any words I would send to Lois Anne had the potential to affect her emotionally. I needed to make sure I surrendered completely to spirit when I asked her important question.

I did just that the next morning. The lengthy poem I received in return spoke of an especially close relationship between Lois Anne and her mother. It described bumps at the end with her care, but most significantly, the poem let Lois Anne know that she had done all she could in the best way she knew how, and that it had simply been her mother's time to go.

I had no way of knowing if any of this information was accurate. In my readings, I got instant feedback from my sitters. In this case, I typed up the poem and sent it by email, hoping for the best. Her reply, when it came a short while later, left me awed at how the spirit world worked.

Dear Suzanne,

I wish I could express my gratitude to you for the release this message brings to me. Mom passed over in March of 2003, and the question has haunted me ever since. The first stanza of the poem speaks of Mom's love for me...I felt her love constantly...still do, but I needed to hear it from the World of Spirit. The second stanza hit upon the "ups and downs" of Mom's stay in a nursing home and in the hospital. The third stanza is all about my taking Mom home as I had promised her I would.

The first portion of the fourth stanza is information I know to be true in my heart, but reassuring to hear it again. However, the words that mean the most to me follow in the last part of the fourth stanza:

> *For your mom is fine now*
> *With the Divine now*
> *Watching every step you take*
> *Every move you make*
> *And thanking you for all you did.*
> *Your selfless action*
> *Brought her satisfaction.*
> *You don't know how much*
> *Your loving touch*
> *Meant to her.*

In the days leading to Mom's death, I physically touched her a lot...but she "touched" me so much more. It was a spiritual experience for me...even the night that she left us. It makes me happy to think that she is watching over me. Most of all, it lets me know that she is "aware of how much I did care."

Each time I read the poem, Suzanne, I cry. Nothing has been so meaningful to me since her passing. My heart is filled with gratitude...

With my love,

Lois Anne

I read her response a second time and shook my head. The poem had been so meaningful that it made her cry? I felt an unexpected surge of love in my heart—as if the poets were saying, "See, we told you so!" I apologized for not trusting them and sent a wave of gratitude for using me in this awesome way to touch other people's lives.

By the time our season of sailing ended, I had found only seven more opportunities to give readings. The number of poems, however, had reached 107, and the poets showed no signs of tiring. Each poem expressed a wise and loving message, but most importantly, each one kept me connected with the unseen realm as I received it. When I arrived home, I felt no trepidation about giving readings to people other than friends and neighbors.

There was one friend, however, with whom I had some unfinished business: Lois Anne.

I had brought through her grandmother and her father, but not her beloved mother. Yes, the poets had passed along some beautiful sentiments, but I knew there was nothing like a face-to-face reading for a sense of connection. I didn't want to rush things and fail to connect with her mother a second time, so I waited until I felt the time was right.

When we finally sat across from each other in my reading room, we shared the same excited anticipation. I reminded her of the kind of feedback I liked to get.

"Let me know if what I say makes sense to you," I said, "But remember not to tell me anything about your mother. It's my job to tell *you* what she's giving me."

I began the reading exactly as I began my meditation sessions, by inviting the spirit world to blend with my energy. Lois Anne's mother must have been standing in the wings awaiting my invitation, for I felt her presence immediately. She wasted no time planting thoughts and images in my mind. Twice I heard the word "bricks," followed by the message that the recent decisions Lois Anne had made were very good.

At first Lois Anne couldn't make the connection between the bricks and the message, but later she informed me that she and Lowell had recently purchased a new home. The final decision came down to two houses, and they had rejected one based on its wood construction. The house they decided upon was made of bricks. She loved knowing that her mother was aware of the decision they'd made and that she approved of it.

I relied on clairaudience when receiving the poems, but the reading for Lois Anne brought through far more visual images than auditory. One clear picture followed another, and each brought a smile of delight to Lois Anne.

"I'm sensing that she liked to bake," I said, "because she's showing me a plate of brownies."

"Always brownies."

"I got the brownies big time."

"Big time," she affirmed.

Her mother went on to show me a small dog that Lois Anne recognized by my description, and a cigar box, which Lois Anne still had. When I described a porcelain vase with flowers on it, she hesitated, unsure. The image was so clear that I asked her to make a note of the vase and get back to me later if she remembered anything more concrete. It would be another week before Lois Anne emailed me to say that she was walking into her kitchen when she glanced on top of the refrigerator and saw her mother's porcelain vase with flowers on it. This "aha" moment made my day, for once again it proved that I could not have been reading Lois Anne's mind during the reading; the information had come straight from her mother.

The reading continued, and I laughed at what I heard next. "Do you know why I would hear "burnt toast?" I asked.

By this time I was used to getting unusual pieces of evidence in a reading that made no sense to me, and I enjoyed them most of all. These off-the-wall words and images often produced some of the best "wow" moments.

Lois Anne laughed. "My mother and I were both really good at burning toast. And rolls."

"Really?" I said. "Because I didn't get just 'toast.' This was '*burnt* toast.'"

Lois Anne nodded vigorously. "I even started a fire one time."

"Remind me not to go to your house for breakfast!" I joked, delighted at the evidential memories her mother was able to share through me.

I closed my eyes and waited for more.

"Now she's showing me a tablecloth. What I see is white, and it has scalloped edges that are embroidered."

"Oh gosh—that's my grandmother's!" Lois Anne exclaimed. "That's her mom. She made the tablecloth. Crocheted, with scalloped edges. She made it. Light colored, yes."

She described exactly what I was seeing. I was amazed at the detail of the image.

"It's in my house, and I use it," she said. "Yes. Yes. Scalloped. It's unique."

Goose bumps covered my arms. "See, your mom's here," I said. "She reaches out now, with one hand to cup your face— a very loving gesture."

I thanked her mother with all the loving vibrations I could muster for giving us such a wonderful experience. My thanks were returned with a tangible flood of love that threatened to burst from my chest.

I shook my head. "Now she's clearly saying, 'I send you signs all the time that I'm around.'"

"Yes, yes." Lois Anne nodded.

"So this visit is merely a formality."

"Yes!"

I concluded the reading shortly thereafter, but neither of us wanted to move. We sat for quite a while soaking up the loving energy that lingered in the room.

Lois Anne was one of the fortunate few who knew in her heart that death was only a transition. I had nothing to prove that day. Her mother was right—the reading had only been a formality, but the opportunity to paint her back to life for a short while was one that both of us would cherish forever.

The next day brought another poem with yet another message of hope, as did the day after, and the day after, and the day after. Lois Anne continued to comment on each one, but I stopped asking questions of the poets. There was no more need to test them. The spirit world had wowed me enough.

Scalloped edges of a cloth,
Fine vases on a shelf,
Pictures of a bygone time—
Treasures beyond wealth.

Images come to your mind
Words you do not know.
It's the evidence they come to hear
From the place where loved ones go.

You bring them back to life for them
For a brief moment they are there.
"I live! I'm here!" they say to them
"I reach out and stroke your hair."

"You cannot see me, yet I'm here.
When you call my name I hear you.
So speak to me and come I will.
Your voice it draws me near you."

A medium two souls unite,
Yet for this there is no need.
For always are two hearts enjoined
Who once on love did feed.

Embrace your loved ones with your heart
Even though they have moved on.
You'll see them once again, please know,
For they're not forever gone.

Just from your sight for now removed,
But much aware they are of you.
So walk this day with lighter steps
For they walk with you, too.

10

First Hand

Word of mouth is the best way to find a good medium.
Along those same lines, a medium should never have to
advertise. That's what they taught me at medium school,
anyway. I took this to mean that if I wanted people to sit with
me, I had to give them something to talk about.

My friends started referring their friends to me, and I
began to get requests for readings from people I'd never met.
When potential sitters asked how much I charged, I hesitated. I
still considered myself a baby medium and didn't feel comfortable asking for money. Still, my time was worth something . . . .

As a solution to my quandary, I considered an idea that had
occurred to me while studying at Arthur Findlay College. I envisioned myself setting up a charitable foundation in memory
of my stepdaughter. Susan was one of the most generous souls
I'd known. A sergeant in the Marine Corps, she didn't earn a
great deal, but she always gave part of her earnings to charity—
especially those for children and animals. In her honor, I decided to ask for donations for my readings and give the money
to organizations that Susan would have supported. It felt good
to know that in addition to reuniting my clients with their
loved ones, others would be helped by the readings as well.

Connie England was one of my first paying clients. We
first met when I spoke to the parapsychology club in The
Villages. During that presentation I shared some of my spirit
poetry. Afterwards I signed copies of my books and answered

questions from those who hadn't wanted to speak up in front of the group. Connie was one of the last to approach me. She had an I-have to-speak-to-you air about her that made her stand out from the others.

She stared intently into my eyes and said, "I write poetry, too."

"That's wonderful," I replied. I intuitively sensed that writing poetry was more than just a literary exercise for her. I didn't have the nerve to tell her that I didn't consider myself a real poet; I merely took dictation.

I didn't recognize Connie's name when she contacted me a few months later to set up a reading, but I remembered her immediately when she showed up at my door. It wasn't her petite size or her curly blond hair that I recalled, but the intensity of her gaze.

I led her to my guest room, where she took a seat across from me. She appeared to be in her early seventies, so I didn't need to be psychic to figure out that there was a better than average chance that both of her parents were on the other side. Still, sitting with strangers had taught me to have no expectations about who from the spirit world would show up or what they'd have to say.

Expectations or not, within minutes I sensed a motherly and fatherly energy, and Connie confirmed that both had passed. I relaxed and allowed them to prove that I hadn't been making assumptions. The details about their ages and the manner in which they'd passed were accurate, as was the evidence I passed along about their personalities.

I sensed the two of them kicking up their heels and asked, "Did your mother and dad like to dance?"

"Yes."

"I picture this back in the big band era."

"Yes."

I had asked Connie before the reading started to let me know if what I said was on track, but to not give me too much feedback. It was my job to paint her loved ones back to life. With her single syllable answers, Connie showed that she was taking my instructions to heart. I didn't mind her brevity. Twenty simple "yes's" were highly preferable to even a single "no."

Pleased with the connection, I sent out loving thoughts to increase the link even more.

"I just had the sense of the sea," I said. "Did your mother like to go to the ocean, or did she live near the water?"

"Yes!"

I then heard a song by Dido that I'd been listening to just the day before. "I'm hearing the words, 'I've still got sand in my toes,'" I said, "so I think your mother is telling me she liked to walk on the beach."

"She loved the sand in her feet."

And I loved feedback that let me know I was right on target.

Connie's father came through with equal clarity. He showed himself sitting at a desk with papers spread across it.

"He's not a manual laborer," I said, "more like a white shirt kind of person."

Connie nodded and I paused, hoping for more specifics from her dad. The next detail came audibly.

"I just heard the phrase 'Nine to five, like a banker.'"

Connie gasped. "He was a banker!"

I couldn't believe it. "That's awesome! Your dad is here!"

The accuracy of the evidence astonished me, but the surprises that morning didn't end with the reading. When I concluded the session, Connie reached into her purse and pulled out a small, framed photo of a little girl. She set it on the credenza beside us.

"That's me," she said, nodding at the slightly faded black and white picture.

"Okay," I said, trying to figure out why she was showing it to me. Often spirits would put the image of a favorite photo in my mind, but her parents hadn't shown me any pictures.

"Do you remember today's poem?" she asked.

I was pleased that she'd been following the poems on my blog. I tried to recall the one I'd posted just before she arrived. Because I didn't actively compose the poems, I usually forgot what they were about within minutes of meditating. I often went back to my blog and read the poems as if for the first time.

Connie must have sensed that I needed prompting. "It was the first one you've written about children."

I blinked in surprise. That morning's poem was #154. Her comment showed that she had read every one of the poems. I thought for a moment and realized she was right. I couldn't remember any others with a similar topic.

I looked again at the photo on the credenza, but failed to grasp what Connie's picture had to do with the poem. She solved the mystery by again reaching into her purse and pulling out a piece of paper.

"This is a poem that I wrote two days ago," she said as she handed me the page. "It's a poem I wrote to the little girl in that picture."

"To yourself?"

"Yes."

I scanned her poem and smiled at its beauty. I envied people like Connie who could knit together perfect word choices and imagery to evoke a particular feeling. If I tried to do the same, the results were stilted. Only when I surrendered and let the Council of Poets do the writing did the poems sound as good as Connie's.

I got up and retrieved the notepad on which I'd written the spirits' poetry that morning. Holding my poem next to Connie's, I compared the two and stared, dumbfounded. Not only were some of the words identical from stanza to stanza, but the overall context of each was the same as well.

Connie's first lines spoke of the innocence of her childhood, and her desire to have that little girl "sing again with glee."

The Council of Poets said,

> *Hear the little children's voices.*
> *So sweetly they do sing.*
> *The happiness that's in their hearts*
> *Has a wondrous message to bring.*

"All things were possible then," Connie wrote in her second stanza. "You can have that once again."

The poets said,

> *Small children are so innocent,*
> *They have not learned to hate.*
> *If you could only turn back time,*
> *How grand would be your state.*

In the third stanza, Connie wrote, "In wonderment you spent your days, seeing things all 'round…"

The spirit-poets equally emphasized what a blessed time childhood is, saying,

> *No fear, no judgment, no disdain.*
> *Just love without condition.*
> *The lives of man would be so blessed*
> *With not a soul lost to perdition.*

Connie's fourth stanza spoke of the loss of innocence that comes with age, and the poets echoed her sentiments with uncanny precision:

> *But as you grow like blades of grass*
> *The weeds they tend to strangle.*
> *Your false beliefs they do the same.*
> *These "weeds" you must untangle.*

Connie concluded her poem by acknowledging with gratitude her recognition of the little girl still inside: "Now off we go to really live," she'd written.

The poets summarized their work in a similar fashion:

> *Go back then to an early time*
> *When thoughts were pure and true,*
> *And you will find the babe's pure bliss*
> *Is what to you is due.*

We stared at each other. My gaze now matched hers in intensity. Were the similarities in the poems pure coincidence? Was their timing coincidence as well? I could tell that Connie was struggling just as I was to understand why our paths had crossed. Surely there was purpose in our meeting. I wondered if she, like I, was coming to understand that there was no such thing as coincidence.

"I think your parents may have had something to do with this," I said. "They obviously knew we were getting together today."

Only then did Connie tell me that her mother had died just one month earlier. It was obvious that her passing was still a raw wound. I sent a silent thank you to the spirit world for allowing me to help Connie to heal.

As she got up to leave, Connie handed me a small white

envelope. Across the front she had written "Love offering" in delicate script. I set it on the credenza and thanked her on behalf of Susan's foundation. The money would be put to good use.

I made it a habit to hug my clients at the door before they left. Their trust in allowing me into their most personal places during a reading created a unique bond that I liked to acknowledge with love. I reached out to embrace her and she returned the hug with a rush of heart-felt emotion that caused my heart to swell.

Connie turned and walked out the door without another word. I stared after her … changed … as she climbed into a large white SUV and drove away.

"I want to hear from my mother," Alice Tarturo told me.

I winced. I usually asked people not to tell me who they wanted to hear from, but Alice didn't give me a chance.

Nevertheless, I sensed a motherly vibration as soon as I closed my eyes and gave Alice several distinct details that followed.

"I don't know anything about that," she said in response to each piece of evidence.

"I don't know what to tell you," I said and exhaled forcefully to clear the doubts. "I just know what I'm sensing."

"I suppose it could be my mother," Alice said, "but I never knew her."

My poker face failed me as my eyes flew open. "If you never knew her, then you wouldn't know if anything I said was right or wrong!"

"That's true."

I shrugged. "Then I guess we both have to trust what I'm getting."

I closed my eyes again, but I got nothing more from the

spirit. After a long pause, I felt a noticeable shift in the energy. A strong female presence came in on my left side where I'd asked those on the mother's side of the family to let me sense them. I passed along several concrete details until Alice finally nodded.

"It sounds like you have my adoptive mother, but some of the things you said match her sister."

This was a new twist—a two-for-one. The more details I gave her, Alice confirmed that I was sensing both women.

"That would make sense," she said, "because the two of them were inseparable."

It seemed that they were inseparable in spirit as well, for I was having trouble differentiating between their energies. I tried a new tack and mentally asked the women to step apart. Only then was I able to tell Alice which spirit I was referring to.

"It feels as if the older sister was the dominant one. I get the strong sense that your adoptive mother would go along with anything she said."

"Absolutely correct."

I focused on my heart and tuned in to what I was feeling. This was when it was most critical for me to keep my mind a blank slate. I had grown up in a loving family. As a baby medium, I naively expected to feel the same kind of affection from all close family members who came through. I was quickly learning that this was far from the case. It would have been easy for me to tell Alice that her mother and aunt sent loving greetings to her. Sadly, the vibrations I felt from the two spirits at my side were anything but warm.

"I'm sorry," I said, "but I'm not feeling a whole lot of love here."

Alice crossed her arms. "Well, you wouldn't," she said flatly.

I bit my lip, and once again realized that a *lack* of affection was evidential in itself.

"I'm hearing a lot of shouting now," I said, "as if this was the norm in your home."

"That's right."

"And I see your mother grabbing onto your arm with quite a bit of force." I reached out my arm and mimicked the gripping motion with my hand. "She would do this quite often."

"Mm-hm."

I shook my head. "Your house was like a dungeon."

"That's what I called it."

"You literally called it a dungeon?"

"Yep."

"That's exactly what I heard. But you escaped at an early age—and that word 'escape' is significant."

"I ran away from home in my teens and never went back."

"Wow." I shook my head, uncomfortable with the negative energy. "This feels really dark to me, and one of the two just said something about 'the twisted twins.'"

Alice nodded and pursed her lips. "That's what everyone called them."

"Those words?" I asked, stunned. "'The twisted twins?'"

"That's right."

"Were they twins?"

"No, but they were always together."

"I couldn't have known that," I said for my benefit as much as Alice's.

I sat quietly a while longer, waiting to sense a feeling of regret or remorse from the women, but nothing of the sort came through.

"I'm sorry, "I said finally, "but I'm not sensing any kind of apology from them."

Alice snorted softly. "I'm surprised they even showed up."

"So why did they?" I wondered aloud. I sat with that question for a moment, and then the answer became apparent.

"We have to remember the whole purpose of mediumship," I said. "It's all about proving the continuity of life. The evidence these two women gave us today shows that like everyone else, they survived the transition we call death, and that the spirit is eternal. The way they came through also shows that we don't automatically become 'angelic' just because we cross over. Their presence with us today may be their first small steps in learning to be more loving."

"Well," Alice said with resignation, "they have a long way to go."

The twisted twins proved a point that I had learned from Anne Gehman—that life was all about the evolution of the soul. We come to this life to learn lessons that help our soul to grow far more rapidly than it could as pure spirit, but even after we cross over we continue learning and growing. It's as if this life is nursery school, and everything we do is preparation for the next level of our soul's education.

I gave a reading shortly after sitting with Alice that brought this point home to both me and my client in a memorable way. Like Alice, Donna Kelly had been referred by a friend. Also like Alice, she appeared happy and well adjusted. I never suspected the troubled childhood that revealed itself when her mother came through from the spirit world.

The evidence I passed to Donna left no doubt in our minds that her mother had shown up for the reading. When her mother spoke of their differences and the way she'd treated Donna, the happy smiles disappeared. Unlike with Alice's adoptive mother, however, Donna's mother soon made it clear why she'd come through.

"She wants you to know how sorry she is," I said, "and I wouldn't say that unless I heard it from her."

Donna sighed. "I've had a hard time forgiving her, but maybe that's why I was drawn to sit with you."

The moment Donna mentioned forgiving her mother, a light bulb went on in my mind.

"I have a poem for you!" I said excitedly. "It's about forgiveness. My guides gave it to me a little while back, but for some reason I just formatted it on my computer today with a picture of some rose petals."

I got up from my chair and motioned for Donna to follow me into my study. "Give me a second to print it out," I said as I fiddled with my computer. "You're supposed to have this."

The file was one of the last I'd worked with, so it took only seconds until the page popped out of the printer. I handed it to Donna and read along with her over her shoulder:

> Forgiveness—the greatest gift
> When used to heal a painful rift.
> Those who harbor pain and anger,
> Who hold for others hardened rancor,
> Hold within their chest a stone
> Leaving them to feel alone.
> Yet when you find it in your heart
> To heal that which does set you apart,
> Then you know the inner peace
> That enters with a great release.
> It comes when you can finally say,
> "I do forgive you on this day."
> Forgiveness doesn't say, "You're right."
> It doesn't carry power and might.
> It's nothing but a touch of grace
> That brushes softly 'cross the face
> And without judgment says, "I know
> That all of us are here to grow,
> And if I send you love, not hate
> Then easier will be your fate.
> For all must pay for what they do.
> You face your actions, this is true.
> But seeing that we all do err

And showing that the love's still there
Then in this way you show to all
That even those who take a fall
Can walk the straight and narrow path
When met with love instead of wrath.

When she finished reading, Donna looked at me with wonder in her eyes. "This is for me."

"I know. From your mother."

"May I take this with me?"

"Of course. It's yours."

She looked down at the poem again, and when she looked back at me, she had tears in her eyes. "I forgive her."

My eyes flooded as well and I nodded, speechless. I recalled my teachers' lesson that a medium served the spirit world as much as the client, if not more so. In that moment, I was filled with gratitude not just for Donna's change of heart, but for the healing her mother received as she stood there with us in spirit and felt her daughter's love.

I had no idea that Donna Kelly belonged to a metaphysical study circle called the Mastery Group. I figured out soon enough that she must have shared the experience with the members of the group, for within days of our session my email inbox filled with requests for readings that all began with, "I'm a friend of Donna Kelly . . . ."

When Margaret Baker took a seat across from me a few weeks later, I asked her the same question I asked every sitter whose name I didn't recognize: "How did you hear about me?"

"I'm a friend of Donna Kelly," she said.

I laughed. "She has a lot of friends, huh?"

Margaret smiled.

She wasn't as talkative as most of the people who came for a reading, so I launched into my preamble about what to expect and the kind of feedback that would help me. Margaret had no questions when I finished my spiel, so I turned on my tape recorder, closed my eyes, and invited her loved ones to gather around.

Almost immediately I sensed a female presence on my left side that I'd sensed in meditation earlier. "Has your mother passed?" I asked.

"Yes."

"Uh-huh." I nodded. "It's as if she wanted to come through earlier this morning, and she was just waiting for us to get started."

I felt a shift of energy to my right.

"I don't know what this is about on the father's side," I said, "but we'll focus over here for now because it's very strong. I feel a very loving presence with this woman. I think you had a very good relationship with your mother. Is that right?"

"Yes."

"Good, because believe me, that has not been the case in my readings lately, and it's significant." I allowed myself to fully experience the sensations her mother was sharing with me. The soothing energy could easily be addictive.

"I love this kind of reading," I said. "I feel happiness and love with her, so that's really good. You're not an only child. I sense at least one or two other siblings, is that right?"

"Yes."

I smiled to myself. Another monosyllabic sitter.

Not all of the details that followed were correct, but there were enough hits to keep my energy high. I turned my attention now to the sensations on my right side.

"I'm sensing a heart problem with your father," I said.

"He did have some heart situations. Yes."

"Again, I'm feeling affection from him, and I haven't felt that from a male spirit lately, so yay! This feels like a man who would not be afraid to show affection and hugs."

"This is true," Margaret said, warming up now. "And hugs, yes."

"Hugs, yes. And I feel a hug for you right now, which I just love. He'd be the kind of dad that would tell stories."

"Yeah."

"Yeah. That's great. And I can sense an affinity—a resonance with your mother. It was a good match."

There was no mistaking the loving energy of the two spirits, both individually, and as a couple.

"I do feel that your father was more talkative—more expressive—than your mother."

"Mm-hm," Margaret hummed, confirming the facts. "He was."

"And he feels like a big man. He wasn't fat, but I sense height and solidness."

"Yes. Very much."

"I see him in a white shirt for his work."

"Always white shirts."

The next image didn't go along with the white shirt, and I cocked my head. "I don't know why, but I just saw him chopping wood. He liked the outdoors."

"He did. We had a camp and he used to cut trees down."

"This is New England," I said, and I swept my arm upward as I saw her father doing. "He's going 'Up here,' and I hear 'Northeast.'"

"Yeah."

The words and images kept flowing with few pauses in between. Margaret confirmed almost all of them.

"And now he just showed me a canoe."

"Oh yes, the canoe."

In my mind's eye I saw a splash. "Did somebody fall in

once?"

"I did. It wasn't off the canoe, but I fell in."

"I just saw a big splash. Off a float."

"Off the dock. I was very young."

"That put a big scare in everybody," I said. My statement sounded obvious, but now Margaret's mother was making a point of expressing how serious the incident was to her.

"'No laughing matter' is what I hear. Your mother was safety conscious. She's the one who would make sure you had a life jacket on."

"Yes, she was very protective."

I shook my head. The scene was now unfolding as clear as a movie in my head. "It's as if I'm right there. There are a lot of trees around, and this is on a lake, not a creek or river."

"That's right."

On and on the details flowed. I felt as if I'd stepped into Margaret's family like a long-lost relative reliving the memories.

"Your father had cancer."

"Yes, he did."

"Yes, he did …."

Her father went on to tell me about an issue that Margaret was dealing with in her life at the present time. I nodded enthusiastically when she confirmed this. "Do you see how they show us that they're aware of what's going on in your life?" I asked.

I got a few more pieces of evidence, but her parents' presence began to fade. I'd held the link for almost an hour and knew I was losing the connection.

"I hope you found the reading useful," I said to Margaret. "I'm going to type up the transcript from the recording, and I'll send you a copy."

"That would be great," she said.

I stood and Margaret followed my lead. She reached into

her purse and handed me a small white envelope with "Love offering" written in script on the front.

I stared at the strangely familiar writing, not quite able to place it.

Margaret must have sensed my puzzlement, for she said, "There's something I'm supposed to tell you now."

Her wording struck me as odd. "What's that?" I asked, suddenly suspicious.

"I'm Connie England's sister."

I blinked once, and when the words sank in, I blinked again. Margaret looked nothing like Connie. I thought back to what she'd told me when we first sat down, and I said now, "You're not Donna Kelly's friend?"

"No. Connie told me to say that. She knows Donna from their Mastery group."

Part of me wanted to protest that I'd been hoodwinked, but a less prickly part immediately sensed the wisdom in Connie's ways. If I had known that she and Margaret were sisters, I would have been influenced by the evidence I'd passed along in Connie's reading weeks earlier.

My mind raced to recall who and what I'd sensed in both readings. Just like when I wrote my poems, I was never fully aware of what I said or wrote. In this case, the transcripts would prove to be priceless in comparing both sisters' sessions. If the details matched, what could be more evidential?

Recording or not, there was one detail that I would never forget from the reading with Margaret's sister.

"Your father was a banker, right?"

"That's right."

"That explains the white shirt, but I had no idea he was so outdoorsy."

"We had a camp in Maine."

"The northeast—" I said, mimicking again the sweeping motion of the arm that her father had shown me. "You and Connie will have to compare notes after I get this transcript typed," I said.

"You can tell her some of it now," Margaret said. "She should be out front to pick me up."

Surprised, I marched to the front door, and sure enough, there was the white SUV parked at the curb.

With Margaret at my heels, I made a beeline for the car. Connie saw me coming and rolled down the passenger's window.

"Part of me wants to be mad at you," I said before she could speak, "but another part wants to kiss you for such a wonderful gift."

"So you forgive me?" she asked.

Normally so serious, the smile on her face transformed her. I thought of the little girl in the photo. There was no way I could be angry.

"Absolutely," I said as I leaned in the window.

"So how was it?" Connie asked.

"I sensed your mother and father again!" I said, excitedly. "Some of the details were the same, but your dad showed me a whole different side of himself. If I'd known Margaret was your sister, I might have been influenced by what I already knew about them, but this just adds even more credibility to what I got last time."

"She knew about me falling in the water at the camp," Margaret said, joining me at the window.

"At the lake!" Connie exclaimed. "I saved her! Mother was pregnant and couldn't jump in. I was twelve years old, and I saved her."

"I saw the splash," I said. "Clear as day . . . and the canoe."

"The canoe . . . ."

We compared more notes until there was no doubt in

anyone's mind that the experiment had been a rousing success. Margaret got into the car and we all waved goodbye as Connie pulled away. I walked back into the house and immediately went to the guest room to retrieve my tape recorder. As I stood beside my reading chair, I stopped and closed my eyes long enough to thank the two sisters' parents for their cooperation with Connie's ploy.

Yes, I'd been duped, but I knew that Connie had nothing but the best intentions at heart. She, like me, was all about proof, and working together, a loving mother and father had given us all the proof we needed.

Thanks to Donna Kelly and friends, the love offerings had added up to a nice little sum of money. When a friend asked if we wanted to support a wildlife rehabilitation fundraiser she was planning, I saw a perfect opportunity.

"What do you think, Ty?" I asked my husband. "We could write the foundation's first check to the wildlife association."

He gave me a wistful smile. "Susan would love it."

I pulled out check number one and wrote in an amount that was greater than any I would have previously given from my personal account. The surprise on our friend's face when I presented her the check warmed my heart.

"We'll list you as a donor in our program," she said.

"That's not necessary," I replied, "but if you do, please note that it's from the Susan Marie Giesemann Foundation."

The next morning I sat down to meditate as usual. I took a few cleansing breaths to relax, then began with my prayers. I went through my ever-growing list of things for which I was grateful, then let my mind grow silent. It wasn't long before I felt the familiar twitch in my finger and picked up the nearby pen and notepad.

Within minutes I had filled two pages with rhyming lines
from the Council of Poets. When the words stopped, I laid
down the pen and thanked them. I was about to open my eyes
and get on with my day, when my head grew unexpectedly
swirly. Surprised, I waited. Suddenly, I heard a familiar voice.

"Hey, Suzanne."

A surge of adrenaline flooded my heart. It was Susan.

When I heard messages in a reading, the words never had
an actual voice. In fact, they sounded so much like my own
thoughts that it was often hard to distinguish them as coming
from a separate entity. This voice, however, was unmistakable. It had been three years since I'd heard my stepdaughter
speak, but the tone and inflection were most definitely hers.

Better yet, I sensed her presence as if she were physically
standing beside me. I wanted to hold onto the moment forever.

Susan's next words—so simple, yet so perfect—brought a
smile to my face.

"Thanks for the check."

Ty and I had made a good choice. Susan had loved all
animals and had a soft spot for anything that was wounded.

I talked with her mentally, telling her how much we
missed her and how grateful I was for all the ways she had
shown us she was around. As I did so, I flashed forward to
sharing this moment with her father. I saw myself saying,
"Susan visited me in my meditation this morning." I imagined Ty patting me on the shoulder and giving me a tolerant,
"That's nice, Suzanne" in return.

I realized this special occasion was no different than any
reading where a loved one came through. If I was going to
prove that Susan had been there, I needed *evidence*.

"I want your dad to believe that you were here," I said to

her silently, "so give me something about your mother that I have no way of knowing."

In reply, our sergeant issued me an order: *"Write this down . . . ."*

I picked up the ever-ready notepad and flipped to a clean page. There I jotted down what I heard next in Susan's distinct voice: three bizarre snippets that were so unique they made my heart soar. If Ty's ex-wife could verify what I'd written, no one could doubt that I had gotten them from any source other than Susan.

I left my meditation space and passed by the study where Ty was doing paperwork. I didn't want to say a word to him until I verified the evidence with Susan's mother. I had shared with her all of the transcripts from readings in which other mediums had brought Susan through for me, and I knew she was a believer. I looked at the clock. It was still early. I avoided Ty and waited anxiously until it was an acceptable time to call. When Angie picked up the phone, I wasted no time getting to the point.

"Susan visited me in my meditation this morning. I finally felt her presence, and there's no doubt in my mind she was there."

"Oh, my goodness," Angie gasped. "That's wonderful!"

"As a matter of fact," I said, looking at the paper in my hand, "she told me three things that are going on in your life now as a way of proving she's around you."

"What did she say?" Angie asked, the anticipation evident in her voice.

I glanced at the short list and looked at the first piece of evidence. It just *had* to be right.

"She said that your cat is sick."

I held my breath. I'd had cats over the years and couldn't remember any of them ever having anything worse than an upset stomach from a hairball. I didn't even know if Angie had a cat, but if she did, and it was sick, that would be more than mere coincidence.

"Oh!" Angie exclaimed. "Mireya has a urinary tract infection! We just brought her back from the vet, and she's on medication."

"Yes!" I said, pumping my fist in the air. *Way to go, Susan!*

"What else did she say?" Angie asked excitedly.

I read the single noun written on the second line. "I only heard her say one word—'ladder,' but I heard it several times. So some incident happened recently for you with a ladder."

Angie only had to think for a moment. "This weekend I was at a friend's wedding at her house. We were all running around looking everywhere for the ladder. Everyone was saying, 'Where's the ladder? Where's the ladder?' Then it just appeared out of nowhere!"

I rocked my head from side to side as I considered that one. Not too many people had any ladder stories to tell, and certainly not as recent as Angie's experience. "Okay," I said, "I'll take that."

"What's the third thing?" Angie asked.

I looked at the list and hesitated. So far we were two for two. In a normal reading, the evidence wouldn't matter quite so much, but the stakes were inordinately high on this one. I had gotten into mediumship solely to prove that Susan was still around. That interest had morphed into an unexpected vocation. This was my big chance to finally prove first-hand that Susan's spirit was with us and that we would see her again. I knew I wasn't being fair to myself, but I felt as if all of my work as a medium rested on this final piece of evidence.

I took a deep breath, then spoke. "She showed me a string of those white Christmas lights in clear plastic tubing. She said that you have them up in your house right now, and that they're there year-round."

It was not the holiday season. The chance that anyone would have Christmas lights up inside their house was slim.

Angie let out a happy laugh. "They run right up the staircase."

I let my head roll back and stared at the ceiling. Three for three. Susan and I had hit a home run. Out of the park.

Thank you, Susan, and thank you, God.

I marveled at how life is filled with ordinary details that by themselves seem innocuous, but added together, they weave a tapestry that tells a most meaningful story to those who recognize the threads. With the simple story of a sick cat, a ladder, and a string of Christmas lights off-season, Susan had given me the first-hand proof I'd been seeking for so long.

I had become a medium to bring comfort to those who had lost a loved one, just as the mediums I sat with had comforted me when I first embarked on this strange and wondrous journey. Alice Tarturo and Donna Kelly had learned important lessons about forgiveness and the soul's journey through life. Connie England and her sister Margaret now knew the joy of knowing that their parents were still around—and all because of Susan.

I said goodbye to Angie and went to share the news with Ty. Susan visited me. I still felt the glow, and her "Hey, Suzanne" echoed in my ears as I walked up to my husband and put my hand on his arm.

11

One Mind

The first time I heard that mediums could give readings over the phone, my first thought was, *How is that possible?* Then I had my session with Janet Nohavec and learned that it was no different than if we'd been sitting together in the same room.

Since then I'd had enough first-hand experiences communicating with the realm of spirit to understand that theirs is a dimension of thought and energy where time and space don't exist. I only had to ask those in spirit to blend with my energy, and they could do so instantaneously. The phone, I learned, was a link only between my client and me. There was never any distance between me and their loved ones in spirit.

My first request for a phone reading came from a woman out of state who emailed me after reading *The Priest and the Medium.* I immediately hit Reply to make sure she understood that I wasn't the medium featured in my book. More than a few folks had made that mistake—a fact I learned after people read the title and asked me what it was like to be married to a priest.

"I wouldn't know," I'd say, laughing at the thought of my husband in a white collar.

Jackie from Georgia assured me that she knew I wasn't Anne Gehman and that I hadn't been working as a medium all my life. My lack of experience didn't seem to matter to her, nor did the fact that I'd never done a reading by phone.

"I want you to help me with some personal issues," Jackie said when I called her later to arrange a sitting.

"I don't normally do psychic work," I told her. "My focus is on bringing through your loved ones from the other side to show you that they're still around."

"Okay, whatever," Jackie said.

Whatever? Her attitude took me aback. Didn't she realize what a great opportunity it was to be reunited with those you thought were gone forever? I couldn't imagine being so cavalier about hearing from a loved one who had died. I thought about telling her that she might want to look for a different medium. Then I realized that she would be the perfect test case for my first phone reading. If she wasn't all that interested in hearing from anyone in particular, she might not be too disappointed if my first long-distance session didn't go well.

I felt an immediate pang of guilt for entertaining the thought of failure. I reminded myself of lesson number one as a medium: the spirit world wouldn't let me down. If anything, it was my own doubts and fears that stood in the way of being a clear channel.

"Okay, let's schedule a phone reading," I said to Jackie, but I emphasized again that I didn't do psychic work.

After I hung up, I frowned, remembering the only difficulty I'd experienced while studying at the Arthur Findlay College. The teachers there had taught us that all mediums are psychic, but not all psychics are mediums. If that were true, then I should have had no trouble with the psychic exercises they laced throughout the week, but struggle I did.

Several of the sessions in England required us to pair up with a fellow student and sense things about our partner's life. If we received information from the spirit world, we were told to ignore it. The exercises were meant to develop our psychic abilities only. Try as I might to read the energy of the person seated across from me, I'd failed repeatedly. I would tell my partner about their personality, their family, their occupation, or their home life, and much more often than not I was wrong. I wanted to throw my hands up in the air and say, "I give up. I'm just not psychic!" But how then could I explain the sense of knowingness I had about so many other things before they happened?

Rather than deal with the frustration, I had simply made the decision to concentrate solely on the mediumistic side of a reading. To me, being able to communicate with those who had crossed over was far more important than knowing if a client would get a new job or find the love of her life. Jackie, however, reminded me that there were plenty of folks out there who were more interested in what was going on in their own lives than in the lives of their friends or family—dead or alive.

A few days after setting up the reading with Jackie, my mother invited me to go bowling. I didn't spend much time in bowling alleys—a fact that was obvious from the funky red rental shoes I placed on my feet. It was fun being with my mother, but the gutter balls got old real fast. After two pitiful games and a third two-digit score rapidly becoming reality, I stood at the head of the alley and prayed, *Help me out here, would you?*

Suddenly, three simple words rang out above the clatter around me: *Be. the. ball.*

I was puzzled for a moment, then I smiled. The Council of Poets had been giving me repeated poems on the topic of oneness. "Everything is connected," they taught me. Granted, they were talking about living things—not a twelve-pound hunk of plastic resin—but I understood what they were getting at. If I wanted the ball to do my bidding, I should become "one" with the ball.

I could feel the eyes of my teammates boring into my back. I needed to give this unusual guidance a try or get heckled for stalling. I stepped off with my left foot and let the ball swing back. As I brought my arm forward, I sent out a direct stream of thought-energy: *I am this black ball. I am going straight down the alley.*

I released the ball and sent it on its way with a final one-ness blessing: *I, as the ball, am going to knock down all ten of those little white pins . . . .*

I watched in amazement as the ball traced a perfectly straight line down the center. It struck the lead pin with exacting precision, sending the other nine pins flying. A cheer arose behind me and I threw my arms up in disbe-lief.

I'd heard of the power of visualization, but was that all that was going on here? When my turn came around again, I tingled with anticipation. Could I do it again simply by *being* the ball?

I am the ball, I thought as I stepped to the line. *I am traveling at top speed down the center of the alley,* I envisioned as I pulled back my arm. *I am knocking down every pin,* I said mentally as I released the ball.

And I—the ball—did just that, resulting in two strikes in a row. My reaction and that of my teammates was utter amaze-ment at this miraculous turn-around. I happily high-fived my mother and the players on the adjoining lanes on my way back to my seat. I sat down, laughing in wonder at this latest wisdom from the spirit world.

Unfortunately, my streak of strikes didn't last. Maybe I was getting tired. Maybe the spirits worried that I might lose interest in mediumship if I got too good at bowling. What-ever the cause, my bowling skills returned to their previous pitiful level for the remaining frames.

Nevertheless, I couldn't stop thinking about those three little words as my mother and I drove home. *Be the ball.* *Be the ball.* Then, like the sun rising above the horizon, it dawned on me that the message wasn't about bowling at all. It was about life in general, and our interconnectedness with all that is.

Back at home I stood in front of my bookshelves and scanned the familiar titles. My personal library had expanded significantly since I embarked on my metaphysical journey. Previously I'd been a voracious reader of fiction. After Susan passed, I set aside almost all novels in favor of books on three specific topics: spirituality, metaphysics, and quantum physics.

The latter was quite a switch for me. In college I majored in foreign languages and shied away from math and science, yet now I found myself reading with great interest about such esoteric subjects as the Heisenberg Uncertainty Principle and the dual wave-particle nature of matter. I had an insatiable need to understand how to explain the phenomena of mediumship and telepathy, and I intuitively felt that quantum physics held the answer.

Through my reading I learned what most mediums already knew: that everything is energy. Everything vibrates, including us humans, and each of us has a unique frequency. That frequency stays with us after we shed the physical body, and it was that energetic "signature" that I had learned to tune into when I gave a reading. By allowing my energy field to blend with that of the spirits, I could sense their personality as if it were my own.

In a giant "aha" moment as I stared at my bookshelves, I suddenly understood that I had been approaching psychic work incorrectly. In the exercises at Arthur Findlay College, I had been trying to read the energy field of my partner as if it were something separate and apart from me, when it was all the same energy. That energy, according to quantum physics, was *consciousness*. We are literally immersed at all times in a sea of consciousness where everything is interconnected.

With the spirit world's message echoing in my ears, I realized that to read another person psychically, I didn't need to go "to" them. I needed to blend my energy with theirs just as I did during a reading. I merely had to *be the ball*, for there was only one "ball." Consciousness was indivisible.

The next day I had to fly from Orlando to Chicago. I had taken on some management consulting after I retired from the Navy, but I now found the work a bit dry. My interest in the business world paled in comparison to my passion for the paranormal. I should have been focusing on the job ahead during the flight. Instead, I sorted through the jumble of thoughts that the experience in the bowling alley had set in motion.

Theoretically, to work psychically I merely needed to expand my energy field mentally, just as I did in a reading, and imagine that field blending with the other person's energy. Since it was all the same consciousness, I should be able to sense the other person's vibrations as if they were my own. Rather than "reading" the other person, I needed to do as the spirit world showed me in the bowling alley and "be" the other person.

I glanced at the passenger next to me by the window. The man was well dressed in dark slacks and a button-down shirt. His dark hair was slightly gray at the temples. He alternated between reading the in-flight magazine and looking out the window. We hadn't exchanged more than a nod of greeting since I sat down, but we were so close that our personal space had been blending for over two hours now. *Theoretically . . . .*

I closed my eyes and took a few deep breaths to quiet my mind. I placed my intention on being successful with my psychic ability and deliberately shifted my consciousness.

I am the man in the window seat, I thought. *We are one.*

I then tuned in to my body, imagining that I was that man in the window seat. *What did I feel?* I listened to the thoughts that came in. *What was on my mind?*

A string of subtle impressions and random facts came to me in rapid succession. When they stopped, I opened my eyes and glanced at my fellow passenger. I felt an overwhelming curiosity to know if what I'd perceived was correct, but I hesitated. I felt sure there was some unwritten rule that psychics didn't do this sort of thing. A person didn't just go up to a stranger and say, "Excuse me, sir, but I was reading your mind and—"

Not only might he think I was a nut case, but it was surely an invasion of his privacy.

Still, I knew I'd never see the guy again.

I argued with myself for a few more minutes until the pilot announced that we had initiated our final descent into Midway airport.

The argument that I would never run into the man again won out.

"Excuse me," I said.

When he turned to look at me, I almost lost my nerve, but my curiosity got the better of me.

"I know this is going to sound strange," I said," but I've been doing some experiments in psychic phenomena, and I'm curious: do you live in a two-story house on the water?"

He cocked his head to the left and studied me for a moment, then his lips formed a crooked smile, and he said, "Yes, I do."

Pleased, but uncomfortable, I grinned and quickly looked away.

Beside me I heard, "What else did you get?"

I turned back, surprised, and found him looking at me

intently.

"Well, I sense that you have a grown son and daughter, and that you're married to their mother —in other words, you only married once, and you've been married a long time."

He nodded thoughtfully. "That's right."

"Mm-hm. And you played on a sports team in high school."

"Baseball."

"Yes, but lately you've noticed some aches and pains, and you've been thinking that getting older isn't so great."

He laughed wryly. "That's exactly what I've been thinking."

"Sorry about that," I said.

"Anything else?"

"Yes. You're a senior executive in your company. You're not the CEO, but you've gone as far as you can up the corporate ladder, and you're beginning to think about what comes next in your life."

He let out a wry laugh. "You're right. It's a family business, and I've gone as high as I can. So, yes, I've been giving some thought as to what's next."

I was thrilled. All of the details I gave him might seem rather ordinary, and I might have been able to guess some of them by his dress or his age, but the thing was—I hadn't guessed. I had *known*. Every detail had been spot-on, and I hadn't heard the information as I did in a reading—I had perceived it as if it were my own life I was looking at.

"Well," I said, "that's all I got, and again I apologize."

"Not at all," he said.

He turned to look out the window and I also looked away. Thankfully, seconds later the plane shuddered from the jarring impact of the wheels hitting the tarmac. The engines roared into reverse and all attention was drawn to the tugging seat belts as we came to a faster than normal stop on Midway's short runway. Neither my seatmate nor I said another word until it came time to deplane, and then it was only a cursory, "Have a good trip," and I scurried off the plane.

My embarrassment was temporary. I knew I would never again try such an experiment. Once had been enough to show me that my theory was correct. Anyone could be psychic if they understood that we are all one.

The next week, Jackie from Georgia called me for her phone reading. Sure enough, I sensed only her grandmother and an aunt on the other side, but Jackie didn't seem particularly excited about making contact with either of them. I felt the same awe every time I sensed the presence of the spirit world, so I had to control myself from blurting out, "Don't you realize how amazing this is to be hearing from people who've died?!"

I could tell that Jackie was still interested in a psychic reading; I sensed her frustration through the line. To her credit, she honored our agreement and didn't ask any questions about her personal life. I hadn't made up my mind before the call if I would try my psychic skills or not, but now I figured the spirit world wouldn't have brought the two of us together if there hadn't been a reason.

"Okay, Jackie," I said, "your grandmother and your aunt send their greetings, but I remember you said you have some issues of your own that you want to know about."

I felt the "catch" on the other end of the line and heard the immediate lift in her voice when she answered, "Well, if you don't mind . . . ."

"Not at all." I said. "Give me a minute to tune in to what's going on with you."

I was nervous, but excited. This wasn't some stranger on an airplane who didn't know who I was. This was a *client* who had a need that she hoped I could fill. My guides' advice rang in my ears: *Be the ball.*

I took a deep breath and thought, *I am Jackie. There is only One Mind.*

The first thing I sensed seemed inconsequential, but if it were true, it would be a good start.

"You live in a house that you own," I told her. "And it's rather small—too small for you, I sense."

"That's right."

"Uh-huh. And you're married, but you don't have any children."

"Yes. I've been married for ten years, and we don't have any kids."

Wow. The goose bumps erupted on my arms. So far so good.

I am Jackie, I repeated. *How do I feel?*

I felt the connection deepen, but I didn't like what I felt. "I sense that you're rather dissatisfied in your marriage. There's a coldness between you and your husband—like a wall between you. You feel frustrated that he's not paying enough attention to you lately."

She sighed and said, "Right again."

Then she surprised me by asking a question: "Can you tell what the problem is?"

Normally I didn't like it when clients asked questions in readings. Questions took me out of my passive state and thrust me into active thinking, but this was different. I didn't have to remain passive; I just had to *be Jackie.*

I said to myself, *Okay, what's the problem?*

I answered without thinking. "It's another woman," I said aloud, instantly alarmed at how I'd failed to filter my response.

Jackie didn't seem to mind. "You're right," she said flatly.

I was stunned—not only because I was right, but because she already knew the answer.

"Can you see who the woman is?" she asked, and I had the

sense that she knew the answer to that one, too.

Again, I didn't think. If I had, my rational mind would have said, *How should I know?* Instead, I simply stated what I immediately knew with unshakable certainty: "It's your husband's mother."

"Yep."

And just as I had on the plane, I saw the whole scenario as if it were my own life, for in that moment it *was* my life.

"Your mother-in-law has been relying completely on your husband lately," I said. "He's giving all of his attention to her and you're feeling left out."

"His father died a year ago," Jackie confirmed, "and now he thinks he has to take his father's place."

I was no marriage counselor, but I intuitively sensed what Jackie needed to hear in that moment. I shared some advice that she seemed to take to heart. She then shifted gears and told me how she'd been struggling between going back to school or looking for a job. She wanted to know what I saw her doing in the future.

That's when I stopped being Jackie. "Your future isn't set in stone," I told her. "You make hundreds of choices every day, and every one of those choices changes the course of your life—some more than others. If I told you what I saw, you might think that's your only choice, and that would not be good. We're all given free will for a reason—to make the best choices we can and to learn from them."

"So you're not going to tell me?" she asked.

I laughed. "Nope. Sorry. I *will* tell you, though, to ask for guidance every step of the way, and hopefully you'll make just the right choices to create the future of your dreams."

I'm not sure that Jackie was fully satisfied with my answer, but I hoped what I said would eventually sink in. As for me, when I hung up the phone I was fully satisfied that I had blended with her energy as well as I could. I learned that giving a reading by phone was no different than sitting with a client in person.

The experience had proved eye-opening, but I didn't see myself doing much psychic work, especially if I wasn't willing to tell people what their futures held. I decided that if I sensed something psychically in a reading that was beneficial to my clients, I would certainly tell them about it. Meanwhile, I would stick to my main mission. Sharing the message of mediumship would remain my focus, but I would always remember the lesson that the Council of Poets made sure I learned:

Filling all of space,
You expand.
Your consciousness could never
Be contained in one hand.

You think you're quite separate—
That alone you do walk.
For your bodies look different,
Varied tongues do you talk.

But the thing that does bind you
Is the stuff which you breathe.
With the Life Force you thrive
And great things you achieve.

This great Force never leaves you.
It's your very own soul.
It joins body and mind
To make One Complete Whole.

12

They Hear You

When I greeted Joanne Olsen at my door, my first thought was, *This isn't someone who would normally go to a medium.* Many who come to see me are nervous, but excited. To me, this woman felt unsure and out of her element. I found myself wondering, *Why is she here?*

I invited Joanne to make herself comfortable in my guest room. She still appeared nervous, so I did my best to put her at ease as I described how the reading would proceed. When I finished my preamble, I held Joanne's hands to tune in to her energy, then said a prayer. We both sat back; I closed my eyes and invited her loved ones to gather around me.

Joanne's mother and father came in with enough force to leave me lightheaded, but the details were sketchy at the beginning. Her parents' energy was so linked that I mistakenly attributed most of the initial evidence to her mother. After repeatedly getting "no's" from Joanne, we figured out that the evidence I was bringing through actually belonged to her father.

As I more accurately described the couple's personalities, I couldn't help but think that these two souls felt almost familiar to me. Either that, or my readings were starting to sound disturbingly similar. It seemed as if I were bringing through more than the usual number of closely bonded couples from the northeast. The woman came through to me as particularly frail at the end of her long life, and she showed me problems walking. Other facts about their lives seemed to mirror recent readings I'd given, and I began to question myself. Were the details I was getting so common that everyone sounded alike?

Thankfully, I also heard and sensed things I'd never brought through from the spirit world, such as the correct information that Joanne's mother had been adopted and had a difficult childhood. Joanne confirmed my statements that her father enjoyed *National Geographic* magazines and had a penchant for counting pennies.

I'd been holding the link with her parents for half an hour when her father gave me the clearest impression of the entire reading. "What I sense with him," I said, "was that he was a good worker, dedicated to the job, and I'm hearing 'banker's hours, like 9 to 5.'"

"Banker!" she exclaimed. "You got it!"

"Thank you, Dad!" I said aloud, but inside my mind was spinning. I'd learned that once the spirit world gets through to you with a good piece of evidence, they'll use it again if the same thing comes up in a subsequent reading. When I'd heard "9 to 5, like a banker" with Connie England two months earlier, that had been one of my best hits to date, but now I couldn't help but wonder, *How many bankers are out there?*

The two spirits' energy receded after that *wow* moment, so I wrapped up the reading by recapping the highlights. I reiterated a thank you I'd received from her mother for Joanne's care at the end, and the message that her mother and father were happy and together on the other side.

"Was there anyone else you'd hoped to hear from today?" I asked.

"Yes," Joanne replied, looking a bit unnerved. "I was hoping to hear from my husband."

I jerked in surprise and did a quick review of the sensations I felt during our time together. I had sensed no other male presence other than her father.

"How long ago did he pass?" I asked, now feeling as if I'd failed, in spite of the strong evidence from her parents.

"Last March."

I sighed and shook my head. Her husband hadn't even been gone a year. While I could tell that Joanne was pleased to have evidence of her parents' presence, I felt sure she would have much rather heard from her husband.

"Let's see if I can tune in to him," I offered. I closed my eyes and waited, but I felt nothing other than the lingering energy of her parents.

My dismay increased when Joanne told me that Homer, her husband of 22 years, had been the love of her life. The energy in the room felt far heavier now than minutes earlier.

"I'm sorry," I said, "but there's no way to control who comes through and who doesn't. I know it has nothing to do with how much a spirit wants to be present. It's most likely a matter of not being able to match his vibrational frequency with mine."

Joanne seemed resigned to not hearing from her soul-mate, but now she made a special request. "I was told that you type up the transcripts of your readings, and I'd like to get one, if I could."

I did my best not to let my face reveal my thoughts. *Who told her that?* I wondered. I'd stopped transcribing each reading several weeks earlier because of the extra time involved. Putting the proceedings in print was a good way to keep track of how my mediumship was improving, and clients enjoyed getting the transcript, but it often took me more time to type them than to do the actual reading.

My to-do list never seemed to let up, but I didn't see how I could say no to Joanne. "I'll try to get to that sometime today," I said. "Do you have an email address I can send it to?"

"It's all right here," she said, and handed me a 3 x 5 card with several lines of handwriting on it.

I took the card and laid it on the credenza next to our chairs. I stood and opened the door to the hallway. Joanne didn't follow me. Instead, she picked the card up and held it out to me again.

"I think you're supposed to read this."

I gave her a puzzled look as I took the card. I scanned the first few lines, but failed to see why it was so important for me to read her name, snail mail, and email address. Then it was as if a light went on in the darkened room as I read the bottom line: "Connie England's sister."

I looked up at Joanne and tilted my head. "You have to be kidding me."

She didn't seem to understand my reaction.

Then I got it: Yes, Connie had set me up again, but it appeared that she'd set her sister up as well. Now I understood Joanne's reticence when she'd first arrived. I'd been right: she wasn't the type who would normally go to a medium. Connie had obviously wanted to see if I'd get the same evidence from her parents on a third try. Now I also understood why the reading had felt so similar to others. It was the third time I'd had this spirit couple in my guest room. There was only one banker out there trying to get through to his daughters, and he'd done a darned good job of it.

I stepped into the hallway. "Ty!" I called out. "Connie did it to me again! This is *another* one of her sisters."

He crossed to us from the kitchen and laughed. "That explains it."

"Explains what?"

Ty described how he'd taken the dogs outside just before Joanne arrived. A car went around the cul-de-sac at the end of our street and dropped Joanne off at our house as he and the dogs walked down the street. He noticed how the woman at the wheel had shielded her eyes as she drove past—an act he found peculiar, considering the thick cloud cover that morning.

Now we both knew who the shady character was: Connie, trying to avoid detection.

I couldn't help but laugh. She took my work as seriously as I did, and knew that by my not being aware that Joanne was her sister, any evidence I brought through would be all the more meaningful.

I looked through the panes on the front door, and sure enough, there she sat at the wheel of her white SUV, now parked in plain view at the curb. I opened the door and marched toward the car with Joanne at my heels. Connie looked up and gave me a guilty grin as I waggled my finger at her. "I can't believe you did this to me again!"

She lowered her head and looked up at me through her lashes. "Do you forgive me?"

"Yes, I forgive you, because I sensed your parents again clear as day, but please tell me this is the last of your sisters."

She assured me there were no others. I then excitedly told her about the evidence I'd gotten during this most recent encounter, including the identical phrase about her father's banker's hours. "There's no doubt it was the same two people," I said. "I'll type up the transcript right away so you can compare all three."

"I didn't tell Joanne anything about the other two readings," Connie said.

We briefly shared some of the more evidential details with Joanne, who still seemed a bit shell-shocked from her experience with me.

"I'm so sorry about your husband," I said again. "Maybe this reading was all about letting you three sisters hear from your parents." I gave Joanne a hug and told her that we could try another time to connect with Homer.

I waved as they drove away, then walked into the house. I was grateful for Connie's gift, but unsettled at my inability to bring through the one person Joanne had wanted to hear from. I knew first-hand the intense longing to find evidence that our loved ones are still around. I'd found that comfort when Susan had come through so evidentially at my first reading, but I'd been unable to give that gift to Joanne.

I thought about Joanne's reading several times over the next few weeks, especially when I ran into Connie and Joanne at a presentation on mediumship. I ended my speech with the suggestion that those in the audience talk to their loved ones with the assurance that their words would be heard.

Afterwards the two sisters came up to greet me. Connie and I hugged and chatted for a moment, but Joanne merely gripped my hand in both of hers. Her eyes said "Thank you," but she seemed unable to speak.

When I questioned Connie later about Joanne's emotional reaction, she explained, "It was your mention of our loved ones hearing us that got to her. Joanne talks to Homer all the time, but she never senses his presence."

I nodded in understanding. It was difficult enough to go through a loss, but even harder without any signs from the other side for reassurance. Joanne had nothing to go on but faith that what I said was true.

Two nights after running into Connie and Joanne, I awoke from a dream for no apparent reason and looked at the clock. It was three A.M. I attempted to go back to sleep, but the dream lingered, niggling at the back of my mind. I rolled onto my back and tried to identify the figure who'd played a starring role. Then suddenly I knew: It was Homer, Joanne's husband.

Still in that hypnogogic state between sleep and full wakefulness, I felt a now-familiar sensation: a presence. I realized with a shiver of excitement that I hadn't just been dreaming about Homer. He was there now. He had used my dream as a way of knocking on the door of my subconscious mind. Now

that he'd gotten my attention, a sense of urgency made it clear
to me that Homer wanted to get through to his wife.

Okay, I thought, and sent him my own clear message
back: *If you're going to wake me up in the middle of the night,
you'd better give me something really good.*

I closed my eyes, and just as I do in a reading, I cleared
my mind and waited for Homer to put something there.

Necklace.

It was as clear as if he'd spoken it aloud. Then, as an added
bonus, he added, *Fingering a necklace.*

I realized I needed to record the words on paper, lest I
forget them by morning. Aware that my movements would
rouse Ty from his sleep, I rolled onto my left side and quietly slid open the top drawer of my nightstand. Just the day
before I'd rummaged through that drawer in search of some
scratch paper. The only paper I'd seen was a spiral notebook
filled with scribbles. I couldn't risk writing over something
and leaving myself with an illegible mess.

Unwilling to turn on the light and disturb Ty, I plunged
my hand into the drawer and smiled in surprise at the seren-
dipitous sensation of soft canvas under my fingers. I hadn't
noticed my old travel tote there the day before, but now I
recognized it by feel. Inside its canvas cover was a full pad of
blank paper. My fingers blindly located a pen with equal ease,
and I was in business.

"Necklace – fingering a necklace," I wrote in the dark.
Grateful to the spirit world for the months of practice they'd
given me at writing with my eyes closed, I silently asked
Homer for more evidence. He demonstrated his eagerness by
giving me one unusual tidbit after another:

"Member of a fraternal org," I wrote. "Either police or Elks."

Then, for some reason, I wrote the next word in all caps:
"ROSES—especially the scent of roses."

I tried to write neatly, giving plenty of room between the phrases so as not to lose what would surely be precious gems for Joanne. I flipped the pages with deliberate care, aware that my movements and the scratching of the pen might awaken Ty. Thankfully, he remained silent. I didn't want anything to interrupt this very special exchange.

I needn't have worried. Homer wasn't going anywhere. In fact, he now seemed downright insistent. *I hear her!* he said, and I underlined the word "hear" in just the way he empha-sized it to me, followed by his very emphatic, *You have to get through to her!*

Don't worry, I thought back to him. *There's no way she's not going to hear about this.*

Homer followed up his message with a few solo words, sent about thirty seconds apart—just long enough for me to write each down on its own line:

"*Hammer.*"

"*Hunting.*"

"*Fishing.*"

During a face-to-face reading, I always ask for confir-mation after each piece of evidence I pass along. Joanne wasn't there to confirm if what I was getting was cor-rect, but I didn't need the feedback. I felt the truth in my heart.

Now on my third page, I wrote a partial phrase as Homer gave it to me. I waited for more, but he seemed to have said what he came to say.

I rolled onto my back and sent a message of my own to Homer: *Thank you so very much for coming, but would you let me go back to sleep now?*

I heard nothing else and drifted off in minutes.

The next morning, I sat on the edge of the bed and read with great excitement the notes I'd written. I knew the spirit world was real, but this was the first time a spirit had come to me in this way. Unlike in a reading, it had taken no effort or request on my part to bring Homer through. The clock told me it was too early to call anyone, so I busied myself getting ready for the day. As soon as it was late enough to place a call without being rude, I dialed Connie England's number.

"Is Joanne still visiting you?" I asked, holding my breath.

"No," Connie replied. "She's back with our sister, Margaret."

I felt a tinge of disappointment. I'd wanted to deliver Homer's message in person, along with the hug that I felt sure he wanted her to have.

I filled Connie in on my nighttime visit. She said nothing in response to my mention of the necklace and the fraternal organization, forcing me to continue reading her my notes. When I brought up the roses, she took in a breath.

"Oh!" she said, "roses were Homer's 'thing'!"

I went over the rest of the list, ending with the final phrase Home had given me. For some reason I'd enclosed it in quotation marks: "Etched in stone."

"Do you know what that's about?" I asked. "Do you know if there's something special on his gravestone or some other reason why he'd give me that?"

Connie remained guarded. "You'll have to ask Joanne about that."

A bit nonplussed at her lack of feedback, I hung up and dialed the number she gave me to Margaret's home. No one answered. I didn't want to state the purpose of my call on an answering machine, so I left a simple message, saying, "Please ask Joanne to call me as soon as she gets in. It's very important."

Finally, she returned my call. Hearing her voice, I took a deep breath and picked up the notes that by now I'd committed to memory. I smiled in anticipation. Unlike when Susan had visited me during my morning meditation, this wasn't a case of having to prove myself and what I'd heard. Homer had been so clear, so present, that it was simply a matter of delivering his loving message.

"You may find this a bit shocking," I said to Joanne, "but Homer paid me a visit in the middle of the night."

Her swift intake of breath revealed her astonishment, but it also hinted at the same hungry hope I'd experienced after losing our Susan: *Are they really not gone forever?*

The line remained silent, and I savored the moment. I knew that nothing could replace the human touch, but in a way, I was about to give Joanne her husband back.

One by one I shared the notes from the pages in my hand. One by one Joanne confirmed them all.

The necklace Homer spoke of was a crucifix that Joanne had given him on the day they were married. It hung on a gold chain that he wore every day during their 22 years together. Joanne informed me that she'd been wearing it since the day he crossed over and that she fingered it all the time, just as Homer had said. "In fact," she told me, "I'm fingering it right now."

She confirmed that yes, Homer had, indeed, been a member of a fraternal organization, but it was the Odd Fellows. When I told her about the roses, it became clear why I'd written the word in capital letters. They truly were his "thing," as Connie said. Joanne described the great pride he'd taken in growing a wide variety of roses around their yard, pruning them, and bringing them to her as a special gift. The note about especially remembering the scent of roses reminded Joanne of a time when she'd been feeling particularly down while driving her car. Her cigarette smoke filled the confined space, until the air was suddenly and inexplicably filled with the scent of roses.

The hammer, Joanne informed me, was in reference to Homer's life's work in construction as a builder. Yes, he hunted, and yes, he fished.

Those details, while meaningful and appreciated, paled in importance when I shared Homer's most critical message: *I hear her.*

I gave Joanne a moment to digest this, then asked her about the final phrase he'd given me. "Why would he talk about something being 'etched in stone'?" Is there something meaningful written on his gravestone?" I asked.

Joanne's voice was filled with wonder when she said, "He wasn't just a builder, he was a master *stonemason.*"

Even though I knew the spirit world is all around us and not off in some faraway place, I still raised my eyes skyward and whispered a heart-felt thank you to Homer and to God for this precious gift. I still don't know why Homer hadn't been able to get through to me when Joanne came for her reading, but he made up for it in a way that neither of us would ever forget.

"How can I possibly thank you?" Joanne asked with palpable emotion. I shook my head on the other end of the phone and told her there was no need for thanks. I was simply the messenger—overcome with gratitude at how the spirit world had used me to reunite these two soulmates, and awed at the persistence of a loving husband who wanted so badly to let his wife know that he was still around.

Look upon the window.
See the shiny glass
Just like that through which you go
When to our world you pass.

It's like a one-way mirror—
That which you look through.
You look but cannot see us
But we certainly see you.

We're with you when you call us.
We gaze upon your face.
But know that while we like this,
Your touch it can't replace.

We miss your hugs and kisses,
The feel of your soft skin.
But all else remains the same for us,
Most of all the love within.

Call us when you want us 'round.
We're with you in a flash—
Brushing by your shoulder
Like the flutter of a lash.

One day you'll know our world up close.
For now you see it not,
Yet you go there in your dreams at night
And by morn you have forgot.

But remnants of us do remain
In your thoughts when you awake.
This gift we leave you in your mind,
A part of us that you can take.

So gaze around you through the glass
That so thinly does divide us.
And know that when you think of us
Much joy you do provide us.

13

Clear Channel

I sat in the chair where I normally gave my readings. Jan
Blythe, my ever-willing friend and neighbor, sat across from
me. Next to Jan sat her sister, Carolyn, who was in town for
the holidays. Carolyn shared our interest in metaphysics and
had had some interesting experiences of her own with the
spirit world. When I suggested that the three of us participate
in an impromptu home circle, she didn't hesitate to say yes.

Mediums have been gathering in private homes for over a
hundred years to commune with the spirit world. Home circles,
named for the arrangement of the chairs, greatly help in the
development of mediumship. When I first took Anne Gehman's
class on the philosophy of Spiritualism, she had recommended
that each student find a group of like-minded individuals to sit
with, but I hadn't found the right mix until now.

With the lights dimmed and our phones turned off, the
three of us discussed the ground rules. We would close our
eyes and ask for those in the spirit world who wished to communicate with us to make their presence known. If any of us
sensed a presence, we would share aloud what we were experiencing. The others nodded and grinned with me in eager
anticipation, not knowing what would happen, but open to
anything.

We joined hands and said a silent prayer, then each retreated into her own inner world. I concentrated on my
breathing, allowing myself to relax into a light altered state as

I did each morning in meditation. We sat quietly for several minutes, then Carolyn's voice pierced the silence. It sounded softer than normal. She made a few philosophical remarks addressed to no one in particular, then grew silent again.

I battled to quiet the questions Carolyn's words brought to mind. Was that a spirit speaking through her, I wondered, or simply her own thoughts?

A moment later I felt the familiar swirliness of a presence blending with my energy, but the sensations in my head were accompanied by an unfamiliar fullness in my vocal chords. I cleared my throat, but the sensation remained. Then I heard an unmistakable command: *Speak.*

Many times the words I hear in a reading can be interpreted various ways, but this word needed no interpretation. Again I battled with my thoughts, trying to remain relaxed and receptive, but at the same time wondering what I was supposed to speak about.

Open your mouth and speak.

There was no mistaking the guidance. And so, as if stepping off a cliff without knowing what lay below, I opened my mouth and said the first thing that occurred to me.

"Good evening."

The voice that came from my mouth startled me. It was far deeper than my own, and very obviously masculine. I could feel Jan and Carolyn's energy bristle and I knew they were as surprised as I was.

Before I could wonder what I was supposed to say next, a thought materialized in my mind. It was just like when a person looks at a tree, and before the words, "That is a tree" take form, the mind already has the concept. I simply opened my mouth and translated the concept into words. As I spoke, the thoughts continued one after the other in burst-like transmissions that I deciphered without consciously thinking.

Similar to when I heard the poems during meditation, the individual words and sentences were lost as soon as they crossed my lips. Thankfully, we'd had the foresight to turn on a tape recorder.

"You must take a back seat tonight," the heavily accented voice said. *"For this we have been coming to you. For this time. To answer questions. To give you knowledge of our world. So, if you have a question, you may ask it now."*

Eyes closed and in another world, I was oblivious to Jan and Carolyn's reaction. They later made me laugh as they described their bumbling and stumbling. To them it was like finding a genie in a bottle, and they repeatedly interrupted each other to ask their most pressing spiritual questions.

"What happens to people who've done bad things after they die?" Jan asked.

"It is a good question," the voice answered in an accent that sounded distinctly Russian. *"They are with like souls. They know immediately they have done wrong in the face of God. It is so apparent in the remorse they feel. It is remorse such as you never have on your earth. This for them is Hell, but they are always surrounded by love. There is nothing but love on the other side, but they do not feel the full force of it until they grow. Do you understand?"*

As this male energy spoke through me, the left corner of my upper lip twitched several times without my consciously doing so. My head was drawn to a position 45 degrees to the left, held there as if by a magnet. The spirit answered several more questions, then the pressure backed off and my head rocked slowly back and forth from left to right.

Seconds later, as if my skull were a divining rod, I was drawn to the equivalent position 45 degrees to the right and my head lolled slightly to the side. It felt as if my face were being caressed by a loving hand. I experienced the same urge to speak, and I stepped off the cliff a second time, happy to be with friends I trusted.

The new voice was unlike any that had ever crossed my lips. Soft and sweet, with an unidentifiable but very proper accent, the tone reflected the soothing, warm energy that filled me with this female spirit's presence.

"*We want to speak, but she tries so hard to keep her consciousness awake,*" the voice said, referring to me. "*So happy are we. You come with goodness in your hearts. We know your curiosity—your desire to see something that amazes you, and this is good. It pulls you like a magnet to us. But this is not a sideshow. There are lessons to be learned, with peace and understanding, filled with love, that you will carry with you when you share these lessons with others, will you not?*"

Jan and Carolyn answered "yes" in unison.

The voice replied, "*It is good to be a messenger.*"

I heard the spirit woman tell us to call her Sally and that we could refer to the male spirit as Boris. I struggled to hold the link as my rational mind rebelled. Was some part of me making this up? The names seemed silly to me. Sally explained that they knew I would have a hard time believing anything they told me. She was right. My disbelief would only have increased if they had called themselves something more alien.

"*Names to us mean nothing,*" she explained. "*We in the spirit world recognize each other by our personal vibration. It is you humans who need to put a label on everything, and so we give you these names as a convenience.*"

I was unaware of time passing, but after answering several more questions, the spirits' presence faded. I sat for a moment to make sure there were no more thoughts coming through. When I opened my eyes, I found Jan and Carolyn staring at me like twin owls.

I laughed self-consciously and shrugged.

"That was amazing!" Carolyn said.

"It didn't sound anything like you," said Jan.

"They just came out that way," I said.

"Even your face changed," Jan said, "and the way you held yourself."

"I felt my lip twitch when the male was speaking," I said, and put a finger to the spot.

"We saw it," Carolyn said.

"That was Boris," said Jan.

I laughed again and tried to recreate the twitching, but my lip wouldn't cooperate.

"I can remember bits and pieces of what came through," I said, "but I was really out of it." I blinked to clear my foggy mind, aware now that I'd gone into a deeper altered state than during a reading.

Jan and Carolyn filled in the blanks of the conversation, telling me that the spirits had given them plenty of advice about their spiritual paths.

"And they didn't cut us any slack, either," Jan said.

"What do you mean?"

"Boris told us that we all have spirit guides, and then a minute later I asked him if I had a spirit guide. He said he had just told us that we all do, and asked me if I hadn't been listening!"

The three of us laughed, then sat silently for a moment. None of us showed any desire to turn on the light and break the spell.

"I did not expect that to happen tonight," I said, then turned to Carolyn. "I thought you were going to have an experience."

"It's okay," she said. "I don't know who that was who spoke through me at the beginning, but it didn't last. What happened instead was really incredible."

I exhaled and shook my head. "And I'm the one who doesn't believe in spirit guides."

Jan threw her hands up. "How can you say that after the Council of Poets give you a poem every day? Today makes how many?"

I sniffed sheepishly. "One hundred sixty-two."

She gave me a look that put me in my place.

I had to remind myself of Jan's words shortly thereafter when I shared the evening's events with Ty. Unusually agitated and still feeling a bit spacey, I invited him to join me for a walk. Ty listened with genuine interest while we walked hand-in-hand through our quiet neighborhood. I knew how strange it had to sound to him as I described the unusual voices and their otherworldly messages, for it sounded equally strange to me. To his credit, he didn't discount what I said. Instead, he encouraged me when I told him that the three of us planned to sit again two nights later before Carolyn returned to Rhode Island.

When we reached the end of our street, we turned to walk back toward our house. Street lamps in each yard provided plenty of light to see our way, but it was the light in the sky that drew my attention upwards. The moon was perfectly round, surrounded by a shimmering halo so large that five moons could have fit side by side inside it. The surreal sight stopped me in my tracks.

"Look at the moon!" I exclaimed. "It's magical!"

Ty agreed.

"I have to share this with Jan and Carolyn," I said, and picked up my pace. It was well after the polite time of night to call a friend, let alone knock on her door, but I knew that the girls were still as keyed up as I was. Sure enough, Jan answered my rapping immediately.

"You have to see this," I said, beckoning her outside.

She joined me in her driveway, with Carolyn close behind.

Other than the butterflies Susan sent me, I wasn't one to put much credence in signs. My rational mind knew that the bright ring around the moon was nothing more than the refraction of light from ice crystals in the atmosphere. Nevertheless, as the lingering effects of the spirits' high energy worked its way out of my system, I couldn't help but stare at the glittering glow and ponder our place in the universe.

Other than telling our spouses about my first channeling experience, I had sworn Jan and Carolyn to secrecy. My inability to fully accept what had happened left me full of doubts. I feared that others would ridicule me or, worse yet, voice aloud my own doubts that I had made it all up. It didn't matter that the poets gave me daily proof of their existence with their beautiful, flowing words. I had a basic problem with trust—not of the spirit world, but of myself. How much of myself, I wondered, was coming through when I spoke, and how much was truly from this Boris and Sally?

Two nights later I set three chairs in a small circle in my reading room. Jan and Carolyn were due to arrive in half an hour, so I shut the door and took my seat. I closed my eyes and asked the spirits to join us again. I asked them to help me to trust this new means of communication. When I finished my prayers, I returned to the living room to await my friends' arrival.

I sat on the couch and picked up a book. Across the room Ty worked on his laptop at the dinner table. Our two dachshunds lay comfortably in their beds in front of the sliding doors leading to the lanai. Suddenly Rudy, the redhead who had proven so sensitive to spirits in the past, sat up and stared beyond me at a point just below the ceiling. He cocked his head to the side, then stood and took three tentative steps toward me. I watched him curiously as he very obviously focused on something that I couldn't see.

"Ty," I said softly. "Look at Rudy."

I kept my eyes on the dog, whose attention was riveted.

"He's looking at something," Ty said.

"Or someone," I said. "This is just like when Rudy saw Susan."

The dog took several more steps forward and jumped onto my lap. He sat back on his haunches and stared fixedly over my left shoulder, a look of great puzzlement on his face.

"Are you seeing this?" I asked Ty, unwilling to take my eyes off Rudy and miss a second of his unusual behavior.

"It's amazing."

"They're gathering," I said. "They're getting ready to join us, as I just asked them to."

Then, on a whim, I decided to try an experiment.

I know you're here, I said in my thoughts. *And I thank you for coming. Now, would you please move from my left shoulder to my right?*

I held my breath as I watched Rudy. A brick in the wall of mistrust I'd built around myself tumbled to the ground as Rudy's eyes and head moved in a slow, perfect track from my left shoulder to my right. In the months to follow, I would remind myself of that magical moment many times. With Ty as my witness and a little dachshund as the spirit world's instrument, my guides left no doubt that their presence was very real.

Sure enough, the spirits were ready and waiting when I ascended to their dimension a short while later in the presence of my friends. The information they gave me that night and in the coming months helped to chisel away at my doubt. Just as with the poetry, their words flowed with grace, beauty, and wisdom beyond my own. And just as with the poetry, they spoke of one topic above all others: love. In her soft, enchanting voice, Sally said:

> *Quite sudden seems the change in this one, and quite frightening at times to her. But can you not see that this has been in the planning for quite a while? And is it not amusing how she is one of the last to recognize it? You need only open your mind, as this one is doing, to the possibility that you are a pure channel of the light of God. Recognize the beliefs that are holding you back. Recognize the beliefs that darken your light, that disallow the full shining of the light of God within you.*

The shifting of energy between Sally and Boris was once again apparent, not just in the position of my head, but in the change of cadence, tone, and accent. Boris said:

> *Never forget why you are here. The purpose of all humans is to develop that aspect of yourselves which is divine. For this you have come. Imagine an earth where all people walked with this understanding. This would be the true Garden of Eden. It is only the misuse of the free will of man that has disturbed this garden. But it can be returned to its natural state through the awakening of all beings, and you can help in this awakening, each in your own way, like tiny seeds that are planted and spread, germinating one by one. It is only the belief that you cannot make a difference that limits you and limits the effect that you can have upon your earth.*

Perhaps it was Rudy's strange actions that raised Ty's curiosity, but one week later when I asked if he'd like to sit in

on a circle, he surprised me by saying yes. We were joined
by Jan's husband, Bob, a quiet, friendly, and unassuming man
with a warm energy that matched his wife's. Like Jan, he had
been raised Catholic, and he now had a growing desire to find
a better fit for his spiritual beliefs. To round out the group,
I invited Lois Anne, my friend who continued to be so sup-
portive of the daily poetry.

All but Ty came with a list of written questions. I handed
out flashlights so they could read their notes in the dim
light. To prevent distraction, I asked that they devise some
kind of hand signal to determine in what order they would
speak. I reminded them that they were there to help raise the
energy in the room—to act as battery chargers for me. The
higher my energy, the stronger the link I could attain with my
guides.

We said a prayer together, then I slowly entered into the
light trance state. It took a full two minutes before the urge
to speak overcame my hesitance. Once they began, however,
Boris and Sally rose to the challenge of answering the many
questions Jan, Lois Anne, and Bob threw at them. My conscious mind could hear the questions, and I forced myself to
surrender any preconceived ideas about the answers. A few
of the questions were of matters for which I personally had
no answers, yet the spirits answered without faltering, with
an eloquence and lucidity far beyond anything I could have
spontaneously produced myself.

I felt self-conscious with Ty there, but pleased that he
wanted to participate. His presence helped to solidify my
own beliefs. If I were making up the voices or the words, my
destroyer captain husband would see right through me. And
so, the words that came from my mouth startled even me
when the heavily accented voice said, *"You, sir, you have not
spoken yet, have you?"*

"Not yet," Ty replied.

There was a pause, then Ty asked, "For those leaders in our world who have murdered millions of people, whom we consider very evil, what happens when they cross over to the other side?"

The question was nearly identical to the one Jan had asked the first night the spirits came through. Ty and I had had this discussion in the past, and I knew he was referring specifically to Adolph Hitler. He had never been satisfied with the Spiritualists' belief that there is no Hell. I had no answer to the question myself, and was as curious as anyone to hear how the spirits would respond. Here are Boris's words:

> *A heavy energy comes with that question, for there is much heaviness in our world when we receive one from your world who has so little advanced.*
>
> *These souls, they are shown their lives immediately. They see their mistakes. They know what they have done wrong. This is the lowest of the low… the lowest vibration that we have on the other side. They remain submerged, you might say, unable to mix with those who have understood love while on your earth plane. They feel nothing of the love that is available to all others. They feel nothing but tremendous remorse. Suffocating remorse.*
>
> *Just try to imagine the most repulsive emotion—regret beyond anything you can imagine—when their eyes are opened to the effect that they had on others. They do slowly learn to understand this. At first it is like a lost cause, for they come to our side not understanding injustice, not understanding the pain they caused to others until they feel the pain themselves— the full pain of what they did to others. The full pain.*

Imagine such a pain.   A long, long period of recovery.   Some will stay there beyond what you imagine as a lifetime.   A very long recovery.   Does this answer your question?

"Yes," Ty replied, "Thank you."
But my guide was not finished:

It saddens us greatly that there are some who never felt the love of God in their hearts, Boris added, for if they did, it would be impossible to harm another.   So completely blinded are some to the God within, to their own soul, their own spirit essence, which is pure love. You cannot give love unless you recognize that this love is your source.   As it comes alive, the more you give love, the more you are able to receive love.

We would later discuss Boris's answer and agree that it was the most satisfying explanation we could imagine.
The heavy energy that Boris mentioned lingered in the room until Sally came in, bringing with her the loving warmth her presence naturally engendered. Her words lifted our spirits as she reminded us of the true purpose of our gathering and of our existence:

We ask you tonight to think with your heart.   Feel with your heart. If the mind truly lies in the heart, and you close your mind, you cannot feel with the heart. You are shutting off your own opportunities to be who you are—to be love.
So we ask you to be open-minded, walking with your hearts fully open. Yes, it does make you vulnerable, does it not? Imagine if all people walked around

radiating love outward and fully accepting it into their souls—spirits infused with love. You would all be glowing, would you not?

Is this a panacea? Is this a false utopia? Could this possibly be a reality? "Not in my lifetime," you say, but what if you entertained this possibility? Roll it around in your mind awhile. Roll it around in your heart. Be open-minded.

We bid you farewell for now, but it is far from the last time, my children. Until the next time, walk as the God-beings that you are and make us proud. We love you so very much.

The presence faded, leaving me sitting alone in my chair. I came out of the trance almost unwillingly, as if swimming to the surface of a deep, deep pond. I opened my eyes and blinked several times. No one spoke. Sally's energy lingered in the air like the soft caress of a feather. None of us wanted to return to the physical world, which felt almost brutal compared to where Sally had just taken us.

Week after week this core group of friends put our chairs in a circle and communed with Boris and Sally. Ty, Jan, and Bob were regulars, but the drive proved a bit far for Lois Anne. I asked Connie England to join us, then one by one we welcomed Gayle, Barbara, and Elizabeth—kindred spirits whose energy told me they were the perfect fit.

Each Sunday evening I would forego my usual glass of wine with dinner and retreat into my reading room to meditate at 6:30. My friends would arrive at 7 P.M. and we would sit immediately, filled with the electric anticipation of hearing what Boris and Sally had to share with us.

We often commented how ironic it was that all present had been raised Catholic except for me. I had grown up in a family with no religion, where talk of God was almost taboo, yet now I opened my mouth and mystical messages flowed freely from my lips. My friends would ask Boris and Sally questions about Jesus and biblical concepts, knowing I was not well schooled in its verses. My guides' replies kept them coming back for more.

Even though my consciousness took a back seat to Boris and Sally, I remained self-conscious about what I was doing, especially in front of Ty. We shared the same military background, and the former naval officer in me struggled to come to terms with this new reality. I couldn't deny the verifiable evidence that came through during my readings, but the channeling sessions were different. I remained highly selective with whom I shared this new aspect of my mediumship.

I worried how Ty was adjusting to yet another change in the woman he married. At first I had merely meditated—a new word in both of our vocabularies at the time. Then I took him with me to consult a medium. The next thing he knew, his wife had written a book about mediumship, which made the unusual subject a regular topic of conversation at social gatherings. Later he watched as I went off to England to study the craft myself, only to come back and hang out my shingle. Now I was sitting in a dark room each week speaking in a trance.

He had supported each step of my strange journey since Susan's passing, but it had to be more than he bargained for.

I didn't realize how fully Ty believed in my work until one morning when he emerged from his study after hanging up the phone.

"That was Don," he said, referring to a friend with whom we'd shared dinner the previous evening.

"Oh, yeah?" I said. "What did he want?"

"He wanted to know why you wouldn't voice your opinion last night when we got to talking about politics."

I smiled, remembering how Don and his wife, Diana, had goaded me, doing their best to get me to join them in complaining about the current state of affairs. I could hold my own in a political discussion. I had a Master's degree in National Security Affairs and had taught political science at the Naval Academy, but my priorities had changed quite a bit since then. When the conversation grew increasingly heated, I simply sat back and listened, completely at peace and happy to let my friends air their opinions.

"What did you tell him?" I asked.

"I said that you're just on a different plane these days."

I smiled, pleased. Don and Diana knew about my mediumship, so Ty's answer was a perfect way to explain things.

"What did he say to that?"

"He wanted to know what I meant, so I told him about Boris and Sally."

I took in a quick breath, aghast. "You actually used their names? Boris and Sally?"

"Yes."

I exhaled slowly and shook my head. Don was a retired corporate executive—about as linear as they came. I'd had no intention of ever sharing my channeling activities with him or his wife.

"How did he react?" I asked nervously.

"He was quite intrigued," Ty said.

I snorted. "I'll bet he was." I knew that anything Ty told Don would immediately be shared with Diana. I looked at my watch. They'd ended their phone conversation five minutes earlier. By now my friends were surely discussing how Suzanne had lost her mind.

Then Ty said, "I told him about the weekly sessions and all the wisdom the guides share with us. I explained that Boris has said that this life is just the blink of an eye to them, and that's changed the way you look at things."

A slow feeling of warmth began to creep into my chest as Ty continued, "And I told him that you can't even fib, and that I sit there week after week and hear how your voice changes and see the physical changes in your body, and I just can't deny that it's real."

Until that moment, I hadn't known for sure what Ty really thought about the channeling. He could tell me a hundred ways that he believed, but to hear him tell an outsider that Boris and Sally were real filled my heart to overflowing.

I leaned in and wrapped my arms around him. As I did so, I found myself staring beyond his shoulder just as Rudy had done with me. There was no one there that I could see, yet I kept coming back week after week to allow these invisible beings to use me as their voice box.

My husband trusted that I wasn't making it all up.

The question was: When would I?

This process of the poetry
Works not when you do try.
For only can we speak to you
When your own thoughts slip by.

It is two different processes—
To receive words and to think.
Like when your eyes you open and close
Or simply let them blink.

You need not do the work at all.
Sit back and let us talk.
For when you try to interact,
It's then we seem to balk.

Do not fear that we won't speak.
It's fear that causes blocks.
Release all doubt and listen …
The trust, our words unlocks.

You see how easily they flow,
Our words, when you relax.
But when you try to get involved
This process you do tax.

For those who see these words, please know
It works the same for you.
The guidance is there waiting
When you know just what to do.

Relax and sit in silence.
You need not think at all.
Just trust that we will speak to you.
Then you will hear our call.

There is no need for effort.
Quite passive must you be.
As in all of life, it works the same:
Just trust and be set free.

14

Back-to-Back

I chatted with my friend Brenda on the phone. She and I had been friends since we were kids. Even though she lived several states away, we kept in touch regularly. We shared the same interest in metaphysics, and after *The Priest and the Medium* came out, she convinced her book club to choose it as their book of the month.

"I have a girlfriend who'd like a reading with you for herself and her husband," Brenda said.

I told her that if the couple sat in on the reading together, I might only sense family members for one or the other. Brenda said her friends wanted individual readings.

At that point in my budding mediumship, I was only doing one reading four days a week. I suggested we set up a phone reading for one of them on a Monday and the other on a Tuesday.

"No, they want to sit with you in person," Brenda said. "Since they'll be driving from Mississippi, couldn't you schedule them back-to-back?"

I did a doubletake into the phone. "They're not thinking of coming all the way to Florida just for a reading, are they?"

"Yep," she said, as if it were the most normal thing in the world. "They read *The Priest and the Medium,* and they want to sit with you."

I laughed nervously. "They do understand I'm not Anne Gehman, right?"

"Of course," Brenda said. "They want to meet with you, specifically."

I shook my head. In my mind, I was still a baby medium. The thought of anyone driving hours for a reading with me added a whole new level of pressure.

While I hesitated, Brenda said, "They've been wanting to go to Florida for a while anyway, and they're going to make a vacation out of it."

Hearing this, I breathed a little easier. "Okay, then," I agreed, "but please tell them that I haven't even been doing this for a year."

"They know that, and they said it doesn't matter."

I was still shaking my head the morning that Jenna and Bob Carson were due to arrive. I went into my reading room an hour before their arrival and sat in my chair to relax and meditate. With my feet flat on the floor and my hands palm-down on my thighs, I sat quietly and concentrated on my breathing. It didn't take long for the stress of anticipation to disappear and be replaced by a soothing sense of peace.

Oh, God and the spirit world, I prayed, *this morning Jenna and Bob are coming a long way to be reunited with their loved ones. Please help me to be the best possible medium between our world and yours. May I give them irrefutable evidence that this life is not all there is.*

As soon as the thought left my mind, my right index finger twitched. The independent movement happened so often just before a poem came through that it no longer surprised me. The twitching that morning, however, was only a prelude.

Soon all four fingers on my right hand were moving in succession from the pinkie to the index finger, drumming rhythmically on my thigh. I opened my eyes and watched with intense curiosity as the fingers drummed, then stopped . . .

drummed, then stopped . . . and I wasn't doing it. The rhythm was unusual, yet strangely familiar. Suddenly, I knew what it was. My fingers were imitating hoof beats. With that thought, my arm erupted in goose bumps—a sure sign that I had received the correct message loud and clear.

I came out of the meditative state and checked the clock. Jenna and Bob were due to arrive in five minutes. I still wasn't completely accustomed to the spirit world using my body to get their messages across, but the sign was unmistakable. I left the reading room in search of Ty. I found him standing in front of the bathroom mirror shaving.

"Ty, the strangest thing just happened in my meditation."

I described the drumming fingers, then said, "I want to go on record right now that something is going to come up in one of the readings today that has to do with horses."

Ty dried the water from his face and pulled the towel away from his mouth, revealing a patient smile. "Okay. Horses. Got it."

Just then the doorbell rang. I took a deep breath, spun on my heels, and went to answer it.

Jenna and Bob appeared to be in their mid-fifties. Both of them were trim and dressed casually but neat. As we exchanged greetings, the honey dripping from their drawled-out words left no doubt that these were Brenda's Mississippi pals.

"Can we offer either of you a cup of coffee?" I asked, as Ty joined us in the foyer.

"Jenna doesn't drink coffee, but I'd love some," Bob said.

"I'll get that for you," Ty said.

I turned to Jenna and said, "Unless you have a preference as to who goes first, we might as well get started while Ty gets Bob his coffee."

She looked to Bob and he nodded his assent.

"Here's something you might enjoy looking at while I'm in with Jenna," I said to Bob. I handed him a small booklet that I'd set on the table in the foyer. The booklet's dark blue cover displayed a large yellow sunflower and the words "Messages of Hope" in large gold script across the top. "These are some of the spirit poems I receive each day while in meditation."

At a neighbor's urging, I'd chosen fourteen of our favorite poems and matched each with an inspiring photograph. Thanks to a generous donation to Susan's foundation from one of my former military colleagues, I was able to print two thousand copies on full-color, glossy paper. The result was a magazine-quality booklet that we distributed to hospitals, hospices, and support groups. Our hope was that the poems would bring comfort to those who were hurting.

Bob thanked me, then Jenna and I retreated to the reading room. I went through my normal explanatory remarks about what she could expect during the session. She had no questions, so I closed my eyes and asked for the spirits to draw near. I immediately felt a male presence.

"It seems almost impossible that I would be drawn so quickly to the right side," I said, "but I feel this spirit right away in the father position. This feels like a male energy over here, so I'll ask right away, is your father on the other side?"

"Yes"

"Wow. That's never happened," I said. "Just whoosh! So he was waiting."

I'd been praying to make contact much faster during my readings, and this was a very good sign that the spirit world was working closely with me to help me improve.

"Let me try to get some evidence from your dad now to let him show us that it's him."

I sensed that her father passed relatively young, around 50 or 60, and she confirmed that he died at 55.

"And I'm sensing that he smoked, and I can feel that it was a heart attack that took him."

"Mm-hm."

I smiled at Jenna's serious demeanor. Inside, I felt like jumping for joy at this excellent start to her reading. I had to remind myself that people came to readings with mixed emotions.

I described her father's work with the sketchy details I was hearing. To me they painted a fuzzy picture that was close, but just enough out of focus that I asked the man to step in closer. As I did so, I heard the word "*furniture*" clear as day.

"I hear a lot of things during a reading, and sometimes they don't mean anything, but for some reason your dad is mentioning furniture. I don't know why he would talk about that, unless it really means something special to you."

Jenna nodded. "That's the only thing I have from him. It's his furniture that's in my house. I've hauled it around for years."

I made a victory fist. "I have a whole list of things I want them to give me, and things they left behind are one of them," I told her. "I just got goose bumps with that, so that's what that was about."

I made a mental note to not dismiss the things I heard simply because I thought they were too mundane, then an image flashed through my mind, "Was one of the pieces a big dresser?"

She shook her head. "No."

I frowned. One of the hardest things I faced was not letting my own mind get in the way and make incorrect associations. Once I was given a good clue, my brain wanted to link it to other familiar thoughts. I released the thought of failure and held onto the link.

"I'm sensing that your father wasn't the neatest person. Is that true?"

"That's true."

"And I also hear '*gambling*,' as if he might have gambled."

"Yes, he did."

This was no mundane piece of evidence, nor was the next word I heard. It came through with distinct clarity, but it caused me a moment's pause. I winced and tried to soften the news.

"And, uh, I'm also hearing '*cheater*.'"

"Yeah." Jenna nodded as if this were no secret to her.

"Wow. So that's probably why his energy feels so heavy. It's almost like he's . . . oh . . . yeah . . . ." I sat back in my chair from the pressure in my chest. "There's an apology here. Does that strike home?"

"Mm-hm."

"And he's reaching out a hand, and I very clearly hear him saying, 'I did love you.'"

"He does reach out to me." Jenna said, and told me how she often sensed his presence.

I found myself rubbing my right leg and had one of those moments of sheer "knowingness" that never failed to leave me with a sense of wonder.

"There was a time when he hurt his leg, and it left him with a limp," I stated with certainty.

"Mm-hm." Again Jenna nodded as she explained, "We were horseback riding and he fell off."

I sucked in my breath and threw out both my hands. "Oh! Thank you! Do you know what you just said?"

Jenna looked understandably perplexed.

"'Horseback riding!' You can ask my husband about this. Just before you and I came in here I told him that somebody who was coming through today had something to do with horses." I described how my fingers had mimicked galloping hoof beats against my leg. "It was him—your dad! Now, *there's* a memory."

"That's amazing."

"Wow."

"I was a little girl. He had that limp for the rest of his life."

"Well, now he's saying that those were good times when you were really little, but that he went off in the wrong direction as you got older, okay?"

"Mm-hm."

"And he's sorry for that. His priorities were wrong." I felt the father's energy grow lighter as I passed along this message. I opened my eyes to see Jenna wiping at tears, and in that moment I knew that the session had helped to heal not just one soul, but two.

After I passed along the apology, her father's presence quickly faded, replaced shortly thereafter by two female spirits. I went on to paint a vivid image of Jenna's mother and her grandmother, which left no doubt of their continued existence in spirit. While I missed the mark with a few of the details, the reading proved to be far better than I'd hoped for. My worries about Bob and Jenna having traveled so far for their reading seemed unfounded. I felt on top of the world as I led Jenna to the lanai where Bob and Ty stood talking.

"Remember the hoof beats?" I said to Ty.

He nodded.

I beamed. "We got the horses. It was a memory from Jenna's dad."

Bob looked at Jenna and said, "She got your father?"

She nodded, but her smile seemed forced.

Bob looked at us and explained. "Jenna has sensed her father several times since he passed, but she still doesn't believe in an afterlife."

His statement contradicted itself, and I gave Jenna a puzzled look.

She shrugged her shoulders. "I want to believe, but I just can't."

"Well," I said, "your reading gave some of the best evidence I've had to date, right down to the physical sensations. I hope it helps to convince you that your loved ones are here and that there most certainly is an afterlife."

Feeling as if I were on a roll, I invited Bob to join me in the reading room. He took the seat across from me, which must have still been warm from Jenna, and I began the session. Unlike the previous reading, I felt no immediate presence. When I finally sensed a female spirit's energy and passed along what I was feeling, Bob had trouble identifying the woman. One "no" followed another, and I found my confidence slipping away.

"She's talking about doilies," I said. "Doilies. Does that have any significance to you?"

"Not with my mother, but Jenna's mother had them all over her house."

I shook my head and tried to tune in better. I gave him three more details. With each one he said the same thing—that the descriptions sounded more like Jenna's family members than his own.

Stunned by how quickly I could go from spot-on accuracy to repeated misses, my energy plummeted. "I'm sorry," I said, "but this just isn't working, and I don't know why. I'm just going to stop right now."

To my relief, Bob didn't seem to mind.

"I understand," he said. "This wasn't for me, anyway. I already believe in an afterlife. I wanted Jenna to have a good experience, and it sounds like she had one."

"She really did—believe me—but I'm disappointed for you, especially after you came all this way. I just don't know what went wrong."

He waved off my apology, then said, "It's funny how so many of the things you said applied to Jenna."

Suddenly I understood. "I think I was still tuning in to her family. This is the first time I've given back-to-back readings, and I must not have made a clear break after Jenna's session."

"Really, it's not a problem," Bob said. "I'm just happy to be here." Then he added, "And I really enjoyed the poetry booklet."

"Take some with you," I said, and handed him a few more from a small pile on the credenza next to my chair. "Please give them to someone who's hurting. That's who they're for."

"We can all use a little of this," he said, holding up the poems.

I called Janet Nohavec the minute Bob and Jenna left. She confirmed my suspicions and said, "There are several things you can do between readings to clear the energy."

She went on to list them, including the simple process of washing my hands and dabbing water on my wrists after a reading. I didn't see the logic in her advice, but I reminded myself that much of mediumship had little to do with left-brained human logic.

"Don't beat yourself up about it," Janet said. "It happens. But remember—your readings are just going to keep getting better and better."

I knew she was right. The incident with the hoof beats left no doubt that I had the potential to bring through ever more accurate evidence. Still, I hesitated a month later when Kathy Hawkins, a neighbor from The Villages, asked to bring a friend for back-to-back readings. I reminded myself that Janet usually gave five readings in a day. I couldn't hope to get better if I limited myself to one. Just like Jenna's father, who had fallen off his horse, I needed to get right back on that horse and ride it.

Kathy and her friend Jean Kelly showed up at my doorstep right on time. Their big smiles and warm energy were typical of residents of The Villages. Every day I was more and more convinced that I'd been drawn to this community for a reason. People joked that there was something in the water that made everyone so happy in my new hometown. I saw it as the Law of Attraction in action. Everyone who moved there did so because they wanted to surround themselves with active, good-hearted people.

My friends and neighbors were not just good-hearted, they were open-minded as well. The public presentations I gave to various organizations around The Villages on the subjects of mediumship and spirituality drew larger and larger crowds. Kathy had heard me speak and wanted to experience a reading for herself.

I asked Kathy and Jean who wanted to go first. They shared excited smiles, then decided on Jean. Kathy took a seat in my living room and contented herself with a book. Jean and I went into the reading room and both emerged an hour later with smiles from ear to ear. I was happy that Jean had gotten some excellent evidence from her loved ones, but all I could think was, *one down and one to go.*

Would I bomb as I had with Bob, or could I achieve the same level of quality for Kathy that I'd just had with Jean?

"I'm going to take about ten minutes to relax and clear the air," I told the women, "so if you'll excuse me, I'll be back in a few."

I left Kathy and Jean chattering away and went into the master bathroom. I turned on the tap and washed my hands in cold water. I dabbed some on both wrists, all the while visualizing myself making a clean break from the last reading. I left the bathroom and walked back past the ladies. I smiled and waggled my fingers at them as I returned to the reading room. Feeling more than a little foolish, I held out my arms and moved them through the air as if dissipating invisible smoke, all the while imagining that this action was clearing the energy.

Finally, I sat in my chair. I mentally thanked Jean's loved ones for coming through, then asked them to completely pull back from the room. I asked my guides to help me in making a clean break and to give the best possible reading to Kathy.

Knowing that I'd done all I possibly could to ensure success, I took a deep breath and invited Kathy to join me. To my great relief, not only did Kathy join me, but her deceased father joined us shortly thereafter. My energy climbed ever higher as Kathy responded with one "yes" after another to the evidence her father brought through me. Janet's tips for clearing the energy from the previous reading had done the trick.

After getting what she needed to hear from her father, his spirit began to recede. I waited, expecting to hear from another loved one. Instead, my head was drawn 45 degrees toward my left side and my upper lip twitched in a way that could only mean one thing.

I couldn't have been more surprised if Santa Claus had knocked on the door.

My guides never failed to show up for our Sunday home circle, but that was for a group of trusted friends. Boris's arrival during a one-on-one session with a stranger threw me off balance. Was I supposed to channel him here and now? How would Kathy react? I could only trust in the knowledge that the spirit world would never set me up for failure.

"I think my guide wants to talk to you," I said, flinching inside as I said the word "guide" aloud.

I sent a mental apology to Boris. If he and Sally had been working with me as long as they said they had, surely they understood the roots of my discomfort.

"You're open to this, right?" I added hopefully, and Kathy nodded.

"Okay, then, I have to go deeper to bring my guide through, so there's not going to be the same interaction as we've had until now." I explained to Kathy that she could talk directly to Boris and ask him questions. I also warned her that another guide might come through as well.

Kathy showed no signs of wanting to bolt for the door to get away from the crazy woman sitting across from her, so I closed my eyes and went deep.

"Good morning," Boris said through me.

There was no mistaking that accent. He began by talking with Kathy about the special bond she felt with her friend, Jean.

"You two are not related to each other by blood, but you have known each other in another lifetime. This you have suspected, have you not?"

"Yes," Kathy replied.

My conscious mind sat in the background, listening to this unusual conversation. Kathy's unexpected affirmative answer allowed me to hold the link and keep the channel open. I did my best not to filter what was coming through. The evidence I'd brought through from Kathy's father proved to me that the spirit world was real, but there was no proving Boris's words. How did I know these weren't my own thoughts?

"Do you have any questions?" Boris asked, and I inwardly winced. If I was making this up, I'd just put myself in a highly vulnerable position.

"Just whatever you can tell me."

This was worse than I'd imagined. How was I supposed to know what was on this woman's mind? And then I remembered: I didn't have to know. I simply needed to release all doubt, and trust.

I surrender, I thought. *I love you . . . .*

My mind was suddenly filled with concepts that were clearly medical. Thoughts and images created a knowingness that was hard to ignore, yet big, red, warning flags went up. I'd heard about the hazards of letting the spirit world diagnose medical problems. There could be ethical or even legal issues involved. I pulled my consciousness back to the surface and opened my eyes.

"Do you have some health concerns?" I asked Kathy.

Her smile disappeared. With her lips knitted together in a thin line she nodded, "Mm-hm."

"Yeah," I said. "Okay. Let's go with that, then. I'm still learning to trust this."

I closed my eyes again. My head moved slightly from left to right, then settled on a position 45 degrees to the right. A soothing warmth descended over me as the unmistakable energy of Sally blended with mine. I gave in to the urge to let her come through.

"Your body is speaking to you with the symptoms that you have. You must pay attention to the signs your body is giving you. Do not suppress them or hide them."

Like a drowning person who sinks over her head, then struggles back to the surface for air, I came back to full consciousness again.

"I'm fighting this," I told Kathy. "I hear medical things and I don't want to get into that. I don't want to be giving medical advice, but you have something going on here." I put my fingers on my stomach to show her a spot exactly in the middle of my torso.

"Not that I want to pay attention to," Kathy said with a small laugh.

I gaped at her. "So that's accurate, isn't it?"

"Oh, yeah." She nodded with great seriousness now.

"Wow," I said, as goose bumps ran up my arm. "This is good. They want to say that you need to seek medical advice, and whatever it is, you need to check it out. I just sense something very much here." Again my fingertips formed a small circle on an area in the middle of my stomach. It was an unusual location for something to be physically amiss.

"Right there." Kathy mirrored my action and put her fingers on the same spot on her body.

My guides were clearly telling me that the problem wasn't actually inside the stomach, so I was confused. What else would cause a problem in a place where there were no other organs? Kathy later shared with me how five years earlier she had fallen against a saddle horn while riding a horse. The fall caused a calcified hematoma. This had been removed by a surgeon, but the golf ball-sized hematoma returned even bigger. I never could have imagined such a scenario, but my guides knew all about it.

"And it's been getting worse, but you've been ignoring it, haven't you?" I said, as the spirits whispered this fact in my ear.

"Mm-hm."

I knew that Kathy had no idea how momentous the reading was turning out to be for me. Philosophical answers to questions during a channeling session were one thing, but the information Boris and Sally were giving me now was *verifiable*.

"Don't ignore it," I said, still fully conscious, and my skin bristled. "Big goose bumps with that. Don't ignore it. They want to say, 'Seek medical advice.' You should have that looked at by a doctor."

"I move certain ways and I get pain there," Kathy said. "A doctor botched it up, and I don't trust anyone with it now."

Boris increased the pressure on my throat and I closed my eyes.

"You should follow your intuition," he said aloud. *"This is your inner guidance speaking to you. Why would you ignore the voice of your own spirit? The body and the mind are so intricately linked. You cannot always heal yourself, and so you must take advantage of the doctors' skill and please have this looked at, but do not wait any longer."*

I bobbed back to the surface. "That's why you're here today—to hear this message."

"That's me," Kathy said, nodding. "I'll do it myself. I'll fix it myself."

"That's why you're here," I repeated, incredulous.

Kathy mirrored my amazement. "I mean, that's me!" she said, shaking her head. "I've been fighting this ever since I had it removed."

I slipped back beneath the waters yet again . . .

You feel more pain, for this in the past has caused you pain. But more than that is the lack of trust and dealing with all of the problems that come with this—the testing, the discomfort, the uncomfortable examinations—but we very strongly advise you to find a new physician in whom you can trust, for this should not be delayed. You have already waited too long, but do not think we mean "too late." No, it is not too late, but it would get much more serious should you wait. So you must push aside this resistance to doctors, this resistance to your own inner guidance that has been gnawing at your brain to fix this. You may have some health challenges in the future. Your friend will hold your hand through this, but you must be the one to push yourself to take care of this problem.

Boris and Sally backed away and I came fully to the surface.

"Wow," I said again as I took a deep, cleansing breath. Kathy hummed thoughtfully.

"This is a first for me," I admitted as I reviewed the past hour's events in my mind.

I realized then why people referred to these unseen helpers as guides. The spirits had guided me to give Kathy just the push she needed to take care of a problem she'd been ignoring. I felt a pang of guilt. Boris and Sally had been with me every step of my journey, it seemed, yet I'd refused to acknowledge once and for all that they were more than just a figment of my imagination. I sent them a mental apology and a wave of heartfelt gratitude.

I scanned my field for any lingering vibrations. I felt nothing but a warm buzz.

"I don't think you're going to get anything else today," I said to Kathy.

She smiled and said, "What more do I need?"

As I heard Kathy's words, I realized that she had voiced my inner thoughts aloud. I had begun the back-to-back readings fearful of failure, only to receive an unexpected gift: the new, but now unshakable knowingness that my guides were very real.

What more did I need, indeed.

Have no doubts and have no fears
For these do hold you back.
It's only from a lack of faith
That you experience true lack.

Back-to-Back

For what is faith, but knowing
That goes beyond belief—
A deep inner conviction
That always brings relief.

So many sit and worry
That they have not enough
That what they want won't come to them,
That life is always tough.

It's those who set aside the worry,
Those who banish all the doubt,
Who find that resting in the Truth
Does bring their dreams about.

What's the Source of this perfection?
What's this Truth of which we speak?
It's the Oneness of the Universe,
Of both the mighty and the meek.

When you realize you're part of this
And step into the flow,
Then Spirit guides your every step
And then perfection you do know.

Then synchronicity is common.
Coincidence is all around.
No longer do you doubt and fear
For the Truth you've finally found.

15

Choices

More than a hundred residents of The Villages showed up at a special session of the energy-meditation class to hear me speak. The presentation was one of my favorites: "Where Science and Spirituality Meet." It was a topic I'd spent two years researching to be able to show how mediumship and all things metaphysical could be explained by the latest discoveries in science. I hoped to help others see that more and more, the paranormal was becoming perfectly normal.

At the end of the presentation I gave each person a copy of the *Messages of Hope* poetry booklet. I suggested that the audience keep the booklet if the poems spoke to them, or send it to someone they knew who was hurting.

Several people came up to me afterwards with comments and questions. One man identified himself as a scientist. He told me he had long believed in paranormal events, but never had a rationale to explain how they could be real. The man made my day when he told me that my talk had brought it all together for him.

As I gathered my materials and got ready to leave, a woman with red eyes and a tear-streaked face approached. She pushed a poetry booklet toward me, open to one of the last pages. Barely able to choke out the words, she asked me to sign that particular page. I had autographed many books since becoming an author, but I hesitated before signing the booklet. I could take no credit for the poetry. The words came from the spirit world; I was merely their scribe.

The woman was insistent. "This poem is for my daughter," she said, pointing at the verses. "She was brutally attacked last weekend. This is for her."

The woman's pain was palpable and my heart ached for her. At the same time, I felt awed at how the spirit world had worked to get the healing words into her hands. My talk that day affected others as well, for I received several emails in the following days that affirmed my work.

"I want to thank you so very much for the wonderful speech you gave on Wednesday," wrote Sandra Moore, a woman I'd never met. "I can't remember being so interested and impressed on any subject—ever. It has been on my mind in a very happy way. What a lovely assurance you gave the audience of everlasting life."

I answer every email I receive, so I replied to Sandra and thanked her for her kind words. Sandra wrote back and asked if she could have a reading with me. I agreed, but told her I had a bit of a waiting list. She asked to be moved to the top of the list. Sensing an urgent need, I agreed, and we set a date one week away.

The following Monday I received another email from Sandra. In contrast to our previous exchanges, her words were noticeably curt. "Please cancel my appointment for a reading. My church teaching is against the practice of mediumship."

I blinked in surprise at the computer screen. Was this the same woman who had written about the reassurance that the thought of everlasting life gave her? I scrolled down to my saved emails file and opened her previous message. Yes, it was Sandra. What had happened between then and now? I looked at the calendar and my eyes fell on Sunday.

I'll never know for sure what caused Sandra to change her mind, but I have a strong suspicion she mentioned her upcoming reading to an authority from her church. I realized then how fortunate I was to have been given the latitude to do my own spiritual seeking growing up. So many of the people who came to me for readings were just learning to accept or reject spiritual wisdom based on how they felt inside, rather than what someone told them to think or believe.

I replied to Sandra and told her that I understood—that she needed to follow her heart. I also commented on the coincidence that following one's heart was the subject of the poem I'd received in meditation just minutes before her email arrived:

> *The Ten Commandments—ways to live.*
> *Guidance to your life they give.*
> *Thou shall not kill; Thou shall not steal.*
> *The truths they hold, in your heart you can feel.*
>
> *But you do not need written rules.*
> *You have your own internal tools*
> *To tell you how to live your life*
> *With greater love and far less strife.*
>
> *It's called your conscience—this your guide,*
> *The compass that you have inside.*
> *And always it will truly steer*
> *A course for you that's plainly clear.*
>
> *When you wish to clearly know*
> *In which direction you should go,*
> *Just tune in to your heart and make*
> *The choice it tells you, you should take.*
>
> *This skill's quite easy for man to hone.*
> *No need for commandments etched in stone.*
> *Just guidance that is always there*
> *That can be trusted to never err.*

I invited Sandra to go to my blog and read the poem—the 244th communication from the Council of Poets. As I hit "send" on my reply to hers, I wondered if she'd notice the irony—that the poem came from a dimension that Sandra wasn't allowed to believe in.

I realized then how far I'd come in my own growth. I wasn't bothered that Sandra didn't believe in mediumship. That was her choice. What did bother me was the lost opportunity for her loved ones on the other side to let her know they were okay. Lesson Number One from Arthur Findlay College was that mediums served the spirit world first. I hoped that Sandra's family members on the other side weren't too disappointed.

The more sensitive I became to people's energy, the easier it was for me to sense when it was "safe" to talk about my work. Fear has a specific vibration, and it was this vibration that so often simmered under the surface when old friends learned what my latest book was about.

A long-time sailing buddy, Nora Ferguson, was one of those who stiffened when we first talked about *The Priest and the Medium*. A true friend, she bought the book and read it anyway. I ran into Nora at a two-day sailing convention in Ft. Lauderdale not long after the incident with Sandra Moore. Nora pulled me aside in the crowded hall.

"I enjoyed your book," she said, "and I see from your website that you're working as a medium now, but I'm just not sure what to believe about all that weird spirit stuff."

I laughed. If Nora had been a student in Anne Gehman's class, Anne would have rapped her on the knuckles for her comment. Anne was adamant that words like "weird," "strange," and "stuff" did not belong in the same sentence with talk of the spirit world.

"Well, hopefully the stories of Anne's experiences gave you some new ways of thinking about the afterlife," I said.

Nora sighed. "I want to believe. I really do. A close friend of mine died suddenly last month. I'd love to think that she's still around, but it's all pretty scary to me."

There it was again—the fear. I smiled and cocked my head. "What's so scary about it?"

"I don't know," Nora shrugged. "I just find it kind of creepy to think of dead people watching me all the time."

"That's not the way it works," I assured her. "They respect your privacy, but when you think about them, it's as if a little light goes on for them. There's no time or space in the spirit world, so when you call on them, they can be at your side in an instant."

"I'd like to believe that about Maria."

"Your friend?"

"Yes."

"I'll tell you what, Nora," I said as an idea came to mind. "Tomorrow morning when I sit to meditate, I'll ask Maria to draw near me just as I would in a reading. If I'm able to sense her, I'll ask her to give me some evidence to prove to you that all this 'stuff' is nothing to be afraid of."

The fearful energy that surrounded Nora when we first began talking had lessened, but it still lingered in her aura. To her credit, she nodded and agreed to our little experiment.

The next morning, Ty walked Rudy and Gretchen on the beach while I stayed in the hotel room to meditate. After saying my prayers and sitting in silence, I received my daily poem. This normally signaled the end of the session, but this day I did as promised and asked to sense Nora's friend, Maria.

I felt nothing. The familiar swirliness that usually accompanied the presence of spirit did not materialize. Just as I was about to open my eyes, however, a short movie clip played out in my mind. I clearly saw a woman walking barefoot toward me on a beach. She stopped and assumed a model's stance—

arms down at her side, one shoulder higher than the other, hips thrust to one side.

I rarely saw the spirits who came to me in my readings. Any physical descriptions I gave came from general sensations such as "tall or short." This image, however, was as clear as a full-color photograph. I knew that I was looking at Maria, even though the image didn't match my preconceived idea of how a "Maria" would look. I had pictured her with dark skin and dark hair, but the spirit in my mind's eye had fair skin and reddish hair.

I held onto the image as Ty and I drove to the convention center half an hour later. I gazed out the side window at the palm trees, lost in thought, when suddenly a word popped into my mind. It was one I'd heard somewhere in the past, but I couldn't place it.

"Hey Ty," I said, turning to face him. "Do you know what 'Petaluma' means?"

He pursed his lips. "Isn't that a town in California?"

I shook my head. "I don't know. It just came to me out of nowhere." Then I smiled. I had told Ty about my experiment. "I wonder if Nora's friend was from Petaluma."

"That would be pretty cool," he said.

I wasted no time in finding out. As soon as we arrived at the conference, I weaved my way through the displays in the vendor's area. I found Nora next to a booth selling life rafts. Her first words let me know that she was as interested in the outcome of my experiment as I'd been in conducting it.

"Did you find out anything?" she asked with nary a greeting.

"I saw a woman that I feel confident was Maria," I said. "But first, does 'Petaluma' mean anything to you?"

"I don't think so."

"Ty says it's a town in California."

Nora tilted her head. "I only knew Maria from sailing, but I'm pretty sure she was from the San Francisco Bay area."

This was getting more intriguing by the minute.

"I wonder if Petaluma is near San Francisco," I said.

I glanced around at the nearby booths in search of a map or nautical chart. Then, in a moment of inspiration, I pulled my iPhone from my back pocket.

"There's a map function on my phone," I said to Nora as I opened the GPS application. When the search box appeared at the top of the screen, I pecked out P-e-t-a-l-u-m-a on the tiny keyboard.

Both of us peered at the map that appeared. A red push-pin pointed to a black dot representing the town. No water was visible in the immediate area. I felt a pang of disappointment, then had another thought.

"Let me zoom out a little," I said as I put my index finger and thumb on the screen and manipulated the image size. There was a moment's pause while the picture readjusted itself, but when it did, the suspense only increased. We could see blue water on the left side of the pushpin, and a large round area of blue to the southeast, but the picture was still too small to read what the bodies of water were.

Nora and I glanced at each other like two lottery ticket holders waiting for the winning number to be called. Once again I manipulated the screen. When the new image appeared, we both drew in a breath. There, in letters twice as big as those that spelled out "Petaluma," was "San Francisco."

"I'll bet you anything Maria was from Petaluma," I said.

"I'll see if I can find out," Nora said.

"It's just too much of a coincidence to hear that word right after she came to me in meditation. It was there in my head— out of the blue—and then you tell me that she was from the San Francisco Bay area? Petaluma could have been anywhere!"

"What happened when you meditated?" Nora asked, now clearly intrigued.

I told her about the vision—how the woman had walked toward me, barefoot, on a beach. "She looked to be about 55 years old, 5'6" tall, medium build, with fair skin, and reddish hair."

Nora's eyes grew wide. "That's her."

I put my hand to the back of my head. "Her hair was straight and full, and cut in a kind of bob." My eyes drifted down the aisle between the display booths and fell on a woman walking towards us. "Her hair was just like that lady's," I said, pointing.

Nora followed my finger and nodded, then both of us said in perfect unison, "*Only shorter.*"

We snapped around and gaped at each other. Before Nora could say another word, I grew suddenly lightheaded. I suffered a moment of dread that something was physically wrong, then I realized what was happening.

"Nora!" I said with such surprise that I startled her. "Maria's here!"

I was not in a meditative state, nor was I dreaming, yet Maria had blended with my energy so well that she might have been standing next to me in person whispering in my ear. No spirit had ever come to me in a non-altered state, let alone in such a public place.

"She used to wear sarongs," I said. "She tied them around her waist like a skirt."

"That's all I ever saw her in," Nancy said, wide-eyed.

"And she's showing me flowers . . . flowers . . . they're all around her face."

Nancy stiffened, then reached in her purse and pulled out her wallet. She fumbled inside, then produced a photo of the woman I'd seen while meditating. The skin, the hair, the height—all were the same. Most striking, however, were the garlands of flowers on the bushes behind her, framing her face exactly as Maria was showing me now in my mind.

"This woman had a heart of gold," I said. "People couldn't help but like her."

"Everybody loved her," Nora said, and I noticed that her eyes were growing red.

As I stood there, eyes open, with people passing by on all sides, I now listened as Maria gave me an important message. It took me a bit aback, but she was insistent.

"Your friend says I'm supposed to hug you right now," I said, and without giving Nora a chance to resist, I stepped close and hugged her. When I pulled back, she reached up and wiped the tears that now flowed freely down her face.

"Maria was famous for her hugs," she said, sniffing. "There wasn't a single time we saw each other that she didn't give me a hug just like that."

"She's right here, Nora. Right now. I feel her! How else do you think I know all these things? Your friend wants you to know she's okay."

Nora nodded. She seemed unable to speak.

I reached out a hand and touched her arm. "Now, I have to ask you. Was that scary?"

She took a deep breath, then shook her head. "No. It was wonderful, but I need some time to digest this."

"Take all the time you need," I said. "And when you're ready, talk to Maria yourself, because she's still around."

I didn't usually push mediumship on people. If the topic came up, I would feel out people's reaction to it. If they seemed uncomfortable, I changed the subject immediately. Nora was a friend, and she had shown an interest in the subject, so I didn't mind suggesting an impromptu reading.

I surprised myself with my boldness, however, a few months later while on a camping trip to Louisiana. We had stopped for the night at a KOA campground and were checking in. I browsed through a rack of brochures in the office while Ty filled out the usual registration forms. The clerk, a short woman as wide as she was tall, had disappeared into a back room to get a map of the campsites. When she stepped back to the counter, a voice in my head said, *You are supposed to give her a reading.*

I looked left and right. There was no one else in the office. I looked back at the woman, whose nametag identified her as Tina, and the thought repeated itself: *You are supposed to give her a reading.*

Ty finished paying and I shared this surprising bit of news with him as we walked outside. He looked at me askance and raised his eyebrows.

"I know, I know," I said, waving my hand. "It's not like this happens all the time, and I don't plan to make a habit of it. Do you mind if I do a reading in the RV tomorrow?"

"Do whatever you think is right," he said.

"That is, if she even agrees to a reading," I added. "She may not be a believer, but that voice was very clear."

Our campsite sat fifty yards from the campground's entrance. As we hooked up the hoses and leveled the RV, I kept stealing glances at the office. Just as we finished setting up, Tina emerged from the office and plopped down on the front step.

"I'm going to go feel her out," I said to Ty.

"Good luck," he answered, sounding a bit doubtful.

I snapped Rudy and Gretchen's leashes onto their harnesses and wandered toward Tina. Our little dachshunds never failed to break the ice with strangers. Sure enough, Tina's face brightened when she saw the dogs, and we struck up a conversation about pets. All the time we talked, my mind struggled to find a way to broach the subject of a reading. Finally, when the discussion began to lag, I took a breath and dove in.

"Do you ever watch the show *Medium*?" I asked, feeling somewhat foolish.

Tina squinted, thought for a second, then shook her head. I waited for her to say something to keep this new line of conversation going, but when she didn't speak up, I felt forced to ask, "Do you know what a medium is?"

"Um, I *think* so," she said tentatively.

I gave her the 30-second version, then decided to go for broke.

"I'm actually a medium, myself," I said and watched the surprise register on Tina's face. When she didn't stand up and bolt for the door, I continued.

"I've only been giving readings for a year," I explained, "and I need all the practice I can get. If you'd be interested in sitting with me, I'd love to give you a reading at no cost."

"For free?" she asked, showing her first real interest.

"Absolutely."

"When could we do it?"

I felt a stirring of excitement. "We want to get on the road by lunchtime tomorrow," I said. "If you could come over to our RV before you start work, we could do the reading while my husband goes to the gym."

In spite of her initial hesitation, Tina agreed. If I truly was supposed to give her the reading, the way was being cleared quite nicely.

We arranged to meet at 8:00, but the next morning 8:00 came and went with no sign of Tina. I was disappointed, but I figured that like Sandra Moore, Tina may have told someone of our plans and was talked out of it. Happily, in this case I was wrong. She showed up at 8:30, apologized for being late, and asked if we were still on.

Ty headed for the gym and I invited her to sit across from me at our RV's dinette. Because she was new to the concept of mediumship, I spent more time than usual on my introductory remarks. I stressed that the point of the reading was to prove to her that life was eternal, and that those she loved who had passed to the other side were still around. When I finished my spiel, I asked if she had any questions.

Tina looked no less nervous than when she first sat down. She wrung her hands and glanced furtively around the RV. Finally she allowed her eyes to make contact with mine and said, "I do have one question."

"What's that?"

She looked away, then settled her eyes on the table before asking in a pinched voice, "Would God think this is wrong?"

The question stopped me in my tracks. With a burst of compassion, I realized what a leap of faith it had taken for Tina to walk through my door. Whatever—or whoever—pushed her to overcome her fears, I asked that force to help me give Tina the best possible experience.

It didn't take me long to figure out that it was Tina's mother who had brought us together. The strong presence allowed me to paint a picture of a woman who truly loved her soap operas, right to the end, when diabetes and congestive heart failure took her. I described the oxygen mask and the wheelchair she needed, and the stack of magazines her mother kept by her chair, along with the heavy yellow ashtray that often overflowed with butts. The spirit woman showed me several events going on in Tina's current life and in the lives of her children—all things that Tina surely knew I could not have guessed.

Tina responded to each detail with only a quick nod or grunt. It was her eyes, however, that showed how much this special contact meant to her, especially when I described the warm hugs her mother used to give her.

Only when the spirit woman had given Tina enough evidence to let her know that she was truly present did she get to the point. She told me that Tina was having a rough go of it lately, made all the more difficult by an abusive husband. When Tina nodded affirmatively in response to the latter, the message was clear.

"Your mother brought us together because she wanted you to know that you're not alone. She's aware of your troubles, and she's right there with you."

By now Tina was crying outright. "I just don't understand this," she said.

"I know, but think about it—I couldn't have known those things about you, could I?"

She shook her head.

"So I hope you can believe that I was actually tuning in to your mother's thoughts and energy. She may be gone from this world, but she's still around you in spirit."

Tina nodded and ran a hand across her wet face. "I really miss her."

I understood that feeling oh so well, and said, "Maybe now you won't miss her quite so much."

I stood and walked Tina the short distance to the door of the RV. I stepped out first, then helped her down the metal steps. When she had both feet on the ground, I said, "Now I want to ask you something."

"What?" she asked with great seriousness.

"Would God think what just happened in there was wrong?"

She blinked back at me. I could almost hear the thoughts whizzing around her head as she compared old beliefs with this new experience. She glanced in the door where I had just given her a whole lot to think about, then she looked back at me.

"No," she said gravely. "I don't think He would."

I nodded, we hugged, and Tina went back to her life—a life that hopefully felt a little bit brighter than it had when she got out of bed that morning.

Ty and I took our time going home, stopping for the night at a state park on the Gulf Coast. When I turned on my computer, I saw an email from one of our neighbors. The list of recipients included everyone on our street. The subject line read simply "Helen Barker."

"Uh-oh," I said aloud.

Helen and her husband Bert lived directly across the street from us, next to Jan and Bob. They were one of the older couples on our street, and had been the first to welcome us when we arrived in The Villages. Bert and Helen watched our dogs one time when we went away for a weekend, and I took care of Helen's beloved orchids when she and Bert took a Caribbean vacation. Helen had been complaining quite a lot lately about feeling old. When I learned that she had recently given away her orchids because they were too much bother, I knew that she had more troubles than she let on about.

"What's the matter?" Ty asked in response to my "Uh-oh."

"I think something happened to Helen."

I opened the email and my heart sank. Sure enough, Helen had suffered a major stroke two days earlier, and it didn't sound good. She was unable to speak and had no use of her right arm or leg.

I immediately thought of Bert. He and Helen doted on each other. At 80 years old, I wondered how Bert would cope with the new challenges he faced. I had the chance to ask him the next day, for when we arrived home with the RV, Bert was standing in his driveway talking with another neighbor.

Ty and I immediately walked across the street and offered our condolences. When we asked about Helen, he smiled and told us she was doing fine. We knew Bert to always be cheerful, and I couldn't help but wonder if he was in denial. The email we'd received sounded as if Helen was far from fine.

"If there's anything you need," Ty said, "Don't hesitate to ask."

"Well, maybe you can tell me something," Bert said, looking straight at me.

"What's that?" I asked, confused as to why he had singled me out.

He pointed at the clouds and said, "Is God really there?"

His question caught me so off guard that I let out a little laugh. Every week I'd watched Bert and Helen leave their house in their Sunday finest. Wednesday nights they attended church socials. From what they told us, most of their friends were fellow church members. Why was Bert asking me about God? Did he know what was going on in my reading room each time an unfamiliar car parked in our driveway?

Thanks to many hours in meditation and to the wisdom of the Council of Poets, I knew that God was there, but I also knew that God wasn't a "He." Standing in Bert's driveway was not the time to discuss the nature of God, but I could certainly reassure him.

"Absolutely," I said as I stepped closer and hugged him. "God is really there. You can count on it."

"I'm not so sure right now," he said through a crack in his perpetual smile.

I thought about Bert's question several times over the next few days. I wanted so badly to knock on his door and have a heart-to-heart philosophical talk, but something held me back. I couldn't help but think of Sandra Moore, who had cancelled her appointment because someone else had told her what to believe. Who was I to tell Bert the same thing?

My mother accompanied me a few days later when I went to visit Helen in the hospital. She knew both Bert and Helen almost as well as Ty and I did after sharing several holiday meals together. Mom and I walked down the sterile hallways, dreading what we'd find. Neither of us could forget the sad sight of my father in that very hospital after he suffered a stroke two years earlier.

The radiant smile that crossed Helen's face when we walked in the room went straight to my heart. Prior to that day, I had felt neighborly towards her, but the instant connection that passed between us in that moment was the unmistakable energy of *love*. Nothing else.

I nodded a quick hello to Bert, who rose from the chair on the far side of the bed. Then, following my heart, I walked straight to Helen and bent down and kissed her. Just as I'd held my father's hand at his bedside, I held onto Helen's hand as we smiled silently at each other. Beaming, Bert offered my mother his chair. She sat beside Helen and took her lifeless right hand in her own.

We did our best to hold a conversation, laughing sympathetically with Helen. Each time she tried to speak, Mom and I would instinctively turn to Bert to translate her garbled words, and each time he responded, "Don't look at me!"

Helen was obviously tired, so we kept our visit short. I gave her another kiss, then hugged Bert on the way out.

"How're you doing?" I whispered.

"I'm okay," he shrugged, and I squeezed him again.

I was buzzing with energy as my mother and I walked to the elevator. My brain felt as if it would burst if I didn't voice aloud the thoughts that flooded it.

"Mom, I know this isn't your thing, but I have to share this with you."

"What, sweetie?"

"When we first saw Bert after Helen's stroke, Bert asked me if God was really there. I didn't feel it was my place to answer him at the time, but it's so clear to me now."

I found myself gesturing—opening and closing both hands as we walked. "God isn't a person like so many people are raised to believe, but God is very real. God doesn't have a body to express love, but we do. That's the way God becomes present when people are hurting—through us. *That* was God there in that hospital room, acting through you, and me, and everyone else who comes to visit. That's God when the neighbors knock on Bert's door with dinner, and when they show their concern in so many other ways. *That's* what I wish Bert could see!"

"Oh, Suzy," my mother said.

"Do you understand what I mean?"

"I *do,*" she said emphatically, and that, to me, was yet another of the miracles that happened so often these days. My mother, for whom the mention of God had always brought immediate resistance, understood exactly what I meant.

I understood, too, that we are each on our own path. The Council of Poets had taught me as much. I understood that there would always be those who put up deflector shields when I talked about talking to spirits. Dogma had a way of doing that to people, but it was all okay. One of our greatest gifts from God was the gift of free will. We were free to choose how we acted and what we believed.

If this Force that we called God expressed itself through us humans, and God was truly infinite, then there were infinite ways for each of us to find our path to God.

So many different paths
Along the road to understanding.
Which one is the right one?
Why, the one on which you're standing.

No matter which you choose,
All lead to the same place.
If indeed your searching takes you
To that special inner space.

It matters not the words
Nor the concepts that you use.
That is the beauty of this life—
You all are free to choose.

The longing that's inside you
Will always lead you on.
A subtle, gentle tugging
That you can rely upon.

It will whisper in the silence,
"I'm here—please notice me."
And when understanding comes to you,
Then finally you will see

That the God that all are seeking
Knows no boundaries nor no limit.
So seek your Source in all that is
And you will find God there within it.

16

Voice of an Angel

The Chicago Body, Mind, and Spirit Expo drew an enthusiastic crowd. After my presentation, a line of people snaked past the table where I stood signing books. I didn't notice the two women waiting off to the side, but when the last person got through the line, the pair approached me. They appeared to be in their early thirties. They had obviously come together, and both smiled at me as if they had a secret.

"We need to tell you what happened while you were speaking," the woman on the left said.

"The energy around you was so high, it was incredible," her friend said. "After you read the poem, I looked at Karen and asked her if you were channeling Archangel Chamuel. I thought it might be him, because you work with so much love."

"And I told Darla that it wasn't Chamuel," Karen said excitedly. "It was Azrael."

I had to remind myself where I was. The Body, Mind, and Spirit Expos drew a crowd whose openness to all things metaphysical far exceeded my own. To these two, talk of archangels with names I'd never heard was as common as discussing the weather.

"I'm afraid I don't know much about archangels," I said, smiling.

This didn't seem to faze the girls.

"Azrael helps people cross to the other side," Darla said.

"He's kind of scary to most people," said Karen, "but it would make sense that the archangel of death would hang around a medium."

I did my best to keep my smile in place and my eyebrows from rising.

I was in Chicago to talk once more about the merging of science and spirituality. The women could have asked me—a former liberal arts major—to discuss the latest discoveries in quantum physics, and I would have been better prepared than I was to talk about archangels. I had only recently added "spirit guides" to my working vocabulary. "Angels" had not yet made the cut.

"Thank you for sharing that with me," I said. "It's pretty cool that you could sense that extra energy."

"The presence was amazing," Darla said.

"You have some incredible helpers working with you," Karen added.

The two turned to leave, and as they did, an unexpected rush of emotion flooded my body. The surge of energy caught me off guard, and for some unknown reason, I found myself looking at the receding figures thinking, *I love you*. It was a strange thought to have for complete strangers, especially two who had given me a message I wasn't prepared to accept. What happened next left me reeling.

With perfect timing in response to my nonverbal thought, Karen glanced back. She looked me in the eye and said aloud, "I love you, too."

Before I could respond, she continued on her way. Stunned beyond thinking, I blindly reached out and grabbed her shoulder.

"Why did you just say that?" I asked as she turned once again to face me. "I only *thought* those words!"

The enigmatic smile Karen flashed me before silently walking away made the whole scene even more surreal.

If it hadn't been for our startling telepathic communication, I might have dismissed the archangel discussion altogether. Thanks to that unspoken *I love you*, however, I couldn't get angels out of my mind. Back at home in Florida the next day, I shared the story with the home circle gang as we gathered for our weekly session. By now, all of us had no doubt there was a spirit world. All present agreed that we had a newfound respect for spirit guides, but the jury was still out on angels.

"Let's ask Boris and Sally what they have to say," Barb suggested.

I reminded her that she or someone else would have to ask the question. Once I entered the light trance state, I was out of the picture.

Since Barb came up with the idea, she did the asking. Only later, as I typed the transcript, was I able to fully digest the answer my guides provided, as Boris said:

> *Of the so-called archangels, this would refer in our reference to a being of sorts, yet with no form—an energy of a much higher order, an energy of pure consciousness that can be in many places at the same time, able to impress thoughts upon those in need of assistance. This energy is very real and available to all of you at all times, and as experienced throughout the ages, these different frequencies of consciousness have differing roles. There are those who help with the sickness, those who help with the grieving, who help with the location of missing objects: differing roles just as you have different roles on your earth plane.*

Sally then added:

This energy that you refer to as angels, to us is a higher order of love. We see them as pure light. It is with their loving energy that they heal. They are seen by many on your plane as light. It is the light that surrounds them when at times they do assume a form, which has resulted in this image of wings—so bright that you would want to shield your eyes. This is the light of love, for the more refined the energy, the closer one comes to the Source of all Love, which is, of course, God.

I found the answer satisfying on an emotional level, but intellectually, I rebelled. To me, angels were the stuff of fairy tales. They made cute little statues and jewelry, but I had no use for those things. Janet Nohavec, Anne Gehman, and every other reputable medium I knew had angel pictures and knick-knacks all around their homes, but when I saw angel displays in gift shops, I always passed them by. Navy Commanders didn't go for all that angel nonsense.

Still, I was intrigued enough to make a special trip to the local Barnes and Noble to learn more about the topic. I started reading my new book in bed that night. It was interesting, but I couldn't help but feel the familiar stirrings of skepticism. I could allow that angels *might* be real, but where was the proof? I turned out the light and closed my eyes. Still unsettled, I prayed for understanding and evidence.

I was only halfway through my new book on angels when Pam Warren came for a reading. Like so many of my clients, I had seen her in the audience at one of my talks, but we had never met. The session started like most, with a few of Pam's close relatives making themselves known. Then I sensed the energy of a female friend. I felt that she had been quite a bit older than Pam when she passed. Upon hearing this, Pam sat up straighter, showing more interest than she had in hearing from her family members.

"She's talking about crystals," I said. "Did this woman work with crystals?"

"She loved crystals. Yes."

"Great!"

"I asked her if she could bring our other friend, too," Pam said.

Hearing Pam's words, I felt a thrill at having brought through someone she had obviously asked to hear from. I sent out feelers for the presence of another friend, and sensed a different energy slightly to the side of the one who had come in first.

"It's another woman," I said.

"Mm-hm."

"She's giving me a name that sounds like Betty . . . it ends in a "y" sound."

"Close enough," Pam said. "It was Tessy."

"I'm not going to get hung up on that," I said. "What I'm hearing from this second woman is that she was somebody who was ahead of her time, and also very wise."

"Yes."

"She had beliefs that other people wouldn't have adhered to."

"Correct."

"You three would hold hands," I said, cocking my head. "I see you sitting with her and holding both hands." The image didn't make sense to me until Pam explained.

"We would pray with her."

"That's it! Ooh. Goose bumps. And now I see cards."

It wasn't the first time a spirit had shown me someone playing cards, but this was different. I looked closer, then said, "These feel like tarot cards."

"Mm-hm."

"Ha!" I exclaimed. "Very good. Wow."

I liked the energy of this second woman. She felt serene, with an advanced wisdom and energy much like my guide Sally's. I listened closely, and the spirit woman spoke to me now in a full sentence.

"'*It's all true,*' she says."

Pam nodded. "Okay."

"That means something to you."

"Mm-hm."

I wanted to ask what it meant, but before I could, I heard another full sentence. Along with the words, I clearly saw the woman pointing directly at me.

"Phew," I said, shaking my head and giving a short laugh at the unexpected message. "Your friend just said to me, '*Angels are real.*'"

I received messages every time I gave a reading. The verifiable evidence that came through before and after these subjective statements from the spirit world gave the messages their credibility. The messages were always something the client needed or wanted to hear, but this was the first time that a spirit's message was directed at me.

Angels are real. It was clearly the answer to my prayer from the night before, but could I believe it? Was this a message from a sympathetic spirit, or simply my own mind giving me words I subconsciously wanted to hear?

I brought my attention back to the task at hand. When I looked across at Pam, I saw with great surprise that she was crying.

"Thank you! Thank you!" she said, dabbing at her tears.

I stared at her, dumbfounded. She was obviously having a "wow" moment, but I didn't understand the extent of it until she explained.

"That was my key word for today!" she cried. "I said before I came in, 'If the word angels comes out today, I'll know it's real.' So thank you!"

Beyond uttering a long "Okay . . ." I was speechless.

Pam, however, had no trouble expressing her excitement and adding to my own. "That's why she said 'It's all true,' because we used to talk about different levels of being and different worlds."

And this, of course, was exactly what Boris and Sally said repeatedly during the home circles and in the poetry—that there were different levels of reality, all vibrating at higher and higher frequencies.

The Council of Poets gave me a poem a few days later to make sure I got the message loud and clear:

Angels may have wings or not.
Just know that they are there,
Watching every step you take,
Of your mind and spirit taking care.

Some of you may call them guides.
It is the self-same thing.
For we do guide you through your life.
Great wisdom do we bring.

"Spirit guides" or "guardian angels"—
What you call us matters not.
What's most important is you know we're there,
For we're the best friend you have got.

We love you unconditionally.
We're always at your side.
And once you truly feel us,
Our love can't be denied.

We're here to give you guidance,
To shout when you're in danger,
To comfort you in times of need.
To us, you are no stranger.

Just call on us at any time.
It's why we do exist.
Ask us anything you like—
To help, we can't resist.

So yes, please know: angels are real.
We're here with or without wings.
It's our great joy to help you through
Whatever your life brings.

It was true—the more I opened my mind to these new realities, the more my prayers were answered. I had come a long way from the woman who used to only believe in things if I could see, hear, feel, taste, or touch them.

Not too long after that reading with Pam Warren, I was shopping for a birthday card in a local Hallmark store. I reached the end of a row of cards and my eyes fell on a display rack of knick-knacks. Even though I could only see it from behind, I was drawn to a small, ceramic angel leaning against a large heart. The angel had a large pair of feathery wings, but it was the words painted in gold on the back of the heart that made me stop and smile. "Give yourself wings to fly."

I hesitated, reminding myself that I didn't do angel knick-knacks.

Then a voice whispered in my ear, "*That's for you.*"

Like so many of the things I heard during a reading, the words sounded exactly like my own thoughts. The message might have come from Pam Warren's spirit friend, or it might have come from

Boris or Sally. It might also, I realized, have come from my Susan. She was just as much an angel now as they were.

I picked up the statue and turned it over, only to see that there were words on the front of the heart as well. These words were also painted in gold, only larger: "Angels believe in You."

I glanced upward, shook my head, and with a happy laugh, I pulled out my wallet.

Epilogue

It was July when I heard the first rhyming words of Poem #1. In the ensuing months, there were only two days that the Council of Poets didn't give me a poem. The first time, I was on our sailboat all day. The seas were so rough that I kept falling out of my chair—not a conducive environment for meditation. The second time, I was over-tired after traveling out of state to speak about the spirit world. I sat down to meditate, but try as I might to quiet my mind, no poem came. I figured the poets wanted me to have a day off.

In July, one year later, I posted Poem #363, then Poem #364, and finally, the momentous Poem #365 on my blog. Lois Anne, the home circle gang, and others who regularly followed the blog all asked me the same thing: *Would the poems continue?* I had no answer. It was up to the Council of Poets. I couldn't help but notice, however, that while the poets found ever more imaginative images and analogies to express their messages of hope and love, there were a finite number of words in the English language that rhymed.

In the back of my mind, I thought that the poems would end with #365, so I was surprised to receive #366 the next day and #367 the day after that. Number 368 followed, but after laying down my pen that third day of a fresh year of poems, I very clearly heard the message that it was time for a new phase.

The next day I sat in meditation as usual with a notepad and pen in my lap, but no poem came. I listened and listened to the empty silence. I thought of the people who would log onto the blog hoping to find a new poem and felt a pang of disappointment, but there was nothing I could do. I couldn't force the poets to speak.

Just as I was about to open my eyes, I heard a message that echoed that of the previous day: *New beginnings . . . a new phase . . . .* I intuitively sensed that this new phase would involve teaching and sharing the messages I had learned from the poetry.

Over the next few days I continued to meditate, but without a poem, I felt an emptiness when I finished. I felt, in fact, bereft. I could still channel Boris and Sally each Sunday in the home circle, but I missed the daily presence of the poets. Followers of the blog expressed the same sense of lack.

Like giving chocolate to someone on a diet, the poets unexpectedly fed me Poem #369 near the end of the month, but none followed for the rest of the week.

I woke up with a sense of anticipation on August 1st. It was my birthday, but best of all, it was my mother's birthday, too. We loved sharing our special day. Mom and I had plans to get together for breakfast, but like every day since Susan passed, my first priority was to sit in silence and feel the presence of Spirit.

I went to my reading room and began my meditation. Just as the session was coming to a close, I felt a completely new energy blend with mine. I sat still, focusing all of my attention on the sensations in my body. Strangely, the energy felt both masculine and feminine. After a moment I heard a voice. It spoke to me in the third person plural, using the pronoun "we" as it explained that "they" were the collective consciousness of all of my guides.

Was this Boris and Sally, I wondered, or the Council of Poets? The voice answered my question as if I'd asked it directly. *"We are the same, but you are to call us Sanaya,"* they said. *"And you should prepare to write, and write, and write as we give you words of wit and wisdom each day."*

As soon as the presence faded, I opened my eyes and crossed the room to where my laptop sat. I went on the

Internet and typed "Sanaya" on Google's search page. I had heard the name Sanaya before, and recognized it now as the first name of the real-life author of several books on channeling. Confused as to why the guides would choose to use this name, I did a new search for the name's origin. The results made me smile. Sanaya, I learned, was a female Sanskrit name meaning, "eminent, distinguished, and 'of the gods.'"

When they first made their presence known the previous Christmas, my guides had told me to call them Boris and Sally. They knew, correctly, that I would have a hard time accepting a more foreign name. Now, having well prepared me to listen to whatever they had to say, they had chosen a most fitting appellation.

On August 2nd, at the point in my meditation when I would normally receive a poem, the strong male-female energy flowed through me again. It happened again on the 3rd, and this time I found my upper torso rocking gently back and forth between the two positions where I normally sensed Boris and Sally. This, I realized, was the "shunting" that Mavis Pittilla had noticed when I physically sensed the presence of spirit for the first time at the Arthur Findlay College.

The rocking back and forth slowed, and my right finger twitched just as it used to do before I received a poem. Sanaya had told me to prepare to write, and I had come prepared. Eyes closed, I picked up my pen and held it poised over a blank notepad. When the words started flowing, I wrote as fast as I could to keep up:

All of the Universe exists for your enjoyment. You are here to play and create, for who are you, but a focus of the consciousness of the Great Creator. It is through your experiences that God experiences God's creations. How else would God be able to play?

Go forth each day with an attitude of playfulness and joy, knowing that all is in perfect order always. Let this be a mantra that falls from your lips at every mo - ment. As you see things you question, say this important phrase again: "All is in perfect order always.". As this phrase becomes part of your creative consciousness, sit back and watch the perfection unfold.

Laugh with joy as you see what happens when you go through your day in harmony with the flow of the Universe. A small coincidence is no longer "luck," but a living example that you are in the flow, part of Cre- ation itself, helping to create the perfection that is Life.

And then go out and play some more, creating yet more perfection. And as you do so, smile. For would not God smile down on God's creation and say, "It is good."?

When the flow of words stopped, I laid down my pen and opened my eyes. The process was the same as receiving a poem. The words were different, but just as beautiful. And then it hit me: a little over a year earlier, the spirit world had tried to give their messages to me in prose, but I had rejected their presence each time, thinking I was making up the words. With their infinite intelligence, they had found a most brilliant way to get through to me—by using poetry.

Now, as I read the beautiful message, there was no ques- tion in my mind as to its source. It had taken a full year and over 365 poems to get through the thick wall of my doubt, but Sanaya had patiently waited until I was ready. She chose my birthday to give birth to her presence.

Those who had visited the poetry blog now had a new connection with the spirit world through Sanaya. Just as with the poetry, we all looked forward to seeing what her message would be each day. As before, it made no difference what was on my mind; those in the spirit world had their own agenda.

One evening in September, while enjoying a party with Jan and Bob Blythe, the conversation turned to Sanaya. All agreed that we enjoyed her words, but that we still missed the poetry. The next morning, when Sanaya started to speak to me in meditation, I noticed that the words were rhyming. Sure enough, an eight-verse poem on the subject of "trust" flowed from my pen in less than five minutes.

The words were beautiful, but immediately I questioned the timing. Had I brought about the poem in response to the conversation with Jan and Bob? The irony of the fact that the poem dealt with trust was not lost on me.

Sanaya went back to feeding me prose the next day, but I couldn't shake my questions. How much of what I channeled came from my own consciousness, and how much came from the spirit world? I prayed for guidance.

Two days after receiving the poem on trust, Sanaya gave me another poem. By this time I had over fifty blog entries of Sanaya's prose. Why were my guides reverting to poetry?

As always, I wrote the words as fast as my hand could move. When I finished, six verses filled the page. I was about to get up and type them as I always did, but I heard another sentence—a title, it seemed: *For One Who is Suffering*.

I had received 370 poems, but this was the first time the poets had given me a title. In the past, I simply numbered the poems, but after I started posting them on a blog, I needed a better way to find them quickly by subject. I would read each poem as I typed it, then give it a name myself. The names never carried the same energy as the poems. This title, how-ever, came directly from Sanaya, and she added a message for me: *Give this one to Bert.*

Having written the poem in a meditative state, I wasn't completely aware of its content. I opened my eyes and read the lines as if for the first time. The title, *For One Who is Suffering*, fit the words perfectly, and Bert, the husband of our neighbor Helen, who was still hospitalized after her stroke, was the perfect recipient of its message:

A fellow human being
Who walks upon the Earth
Feels the same emotions
Which you have felt from birth.

You think that you're alone
As you struggle and you toil,
But all do face the same great tests
As they walk upon the soil.

No human is exempt from pain.
No one does go without
The sorrows and the loss you feel—
Of this there is no doubt.

So when you face a challenge great,
Just know you're not alone.
Help is there awaiting you
By those who also pain have known.

Pull not inside and hide your fears
When worries come apace.
Turn instead to others,
Then your troubles you can face.

Your world is filled with loving souls
Who walk the self-same path as you.
God's gift to man in human form—
Love that comes to see you through.

I immediately got up and typed the poem on my laptop. I formatted it and printed it on a sheet of stationery adorned with pastel butterflies that framed the poem. Finally, I pulled out a blank piece of paper and penned a handwritten note:

Dear Bert,

You asked me some time back if God is really there. I believe He is. This morning in my prayers I heard the attached poem and wrote it down. I feel it's for you.

With love,
Suzanne

Knowing of Bert's strong link with his church, I chose my words carefully. I deliberately used the word "prayers," rather than "meditation." I didn't explain that the poem had come to me nonstop, ː ı mere minutes. I signed the note, then re-read the poem. I realized as I placed the letter and the poem in a large yellow envelope that the verses applied to Helen just as much as to Bert. I would have liked for both of them to know the poem's source, but the only thing that really mattered was that it helped to ease their pain.

"Want to go for a walk?" I said to Rudy and Gretchen as I headed for the door. Their tails wagged in unison as I snapped on their leads. It was not yet 8:00 in the morning. Even if it had been much later, I had no intention of giving the poem directly to Bert. The words on the paper would express the answer to his question about God perfectly without the need for a face-to-face discussion about dogma.

Armed with the envelope and a piece of tape, the three of us headed across the street. I approached Bert's porch and was about to affix the envelope to the door, when it opened. Bert greeted me with his usual wide smile.

"Did you come for cookies?" he asked, looking down at the dogs. He reached over to a table in the foyer and produced two bone-shaped dog biscuits. If Bert had his way, our wiener dogs would turn into little stuffed sausages.

"Thank you," I said, and we watched as Rudy and Gretchen crunched on the cookies. Bert made no mention that it was awfully early to be bringing the dogs over for treats.

When they finished eating, Rudy began jumping at Bert's knee. Gretchen sniffed the floor like a vacuum cleaner.

"Come on, you guys," I said, pulling them toward the street. As I turned to go, I held out the yellow envelope. "This is for you," I said with a smile. Bert took the poem and I headed off.

Normally, when Ty and I walked the dogs, we followed the same route. We would walk to the end of our curved street, then come back via a shorter street that bisected ours halfway. This morning, for some reason, I turned down the shorter street first and walked the route in reverse. Only in hindsight did I recognize the divine timing.

As I walked toward our house, I glanced up and saw Bert's car driving toward me.

I felt sure that he had opened the envelope by now and read its contents. I wondered if he would stop and comment on it. Sure enough, the car slowed. I pulled Rudy and Gretchen well clear of the wheels as he stopped beside us. The passenger window whirred open and I leaned in. The first thing I saw was the yellow envelope lying on the seat.

Silently I looked across at Bert.

"That was for Helen, too," he said without preamble.

"I thought the same thing," I replied, then added, "I hope you'll read it to her."

"I will," he said, nodding seriously.

And then, in a moment in which time seemed to slow, he reached under the envelope and pulled out a small, glossy booklet. The brilliant blue cover with the bright yellow sunflower didn't immediately register in my brain, but the words *Messages of Hope* spelled out in gold letters across the top made me swallow in surprise.

"I've been reading her one of these poems every day," Bert said, before I could say a word.

"You've been reading Helen those poems?" I stuttered.

"Yeah. I don't know where I got them, but they're really nice, just like this one." He patted the envelope.

"Bert!" I exclaimed as I took the booklet from his hand. "It's the same thing. The same Source. These are my poems, but they're not really mine. They came to me in meditation."

"They're yours?"

"Yes! Look." I opened to the inside cover and put my finger on my name.

Bert's eyes grew wide. "I never saw that."

"Well, read it when you get to the hospital and you'll find out how I got those poems. Then read inside the back cover as well," I said, now pointing at Susan's picture, to whom the booklet was dedicated.

In an uncharacteristic display of affection, Bert reached across the seat and gripped my hand tightly in his. "I will," he said emphatically.

I stepped back and he drove off, leaving me staring after the car. I realized then that if I hadn't walked our normal route in reverse, I would have missed Bert, and I never would have seen that he had the booklet.

I raised my face to the sky and looked at the clouds, tinged orange by the rising sun.

"Thank you, thank you, thank you," I said, as tears flowed down my face.

And standing there in the middle of my street, I heard the words: *It is a collaborative effort. Do you see how it heals?*

Then and there, I knew my prayers had been answered yet again. I had asked for guidance to understand how the spirit world worked through me, worried that some of what came through was influenced by my own consciousness. Now they repeated themselves again: *It is a collaborative effort, and it's okay.*

I thought of Bert reading the poem to Helen, one who was suffering, and I knew that the voice was right. It was okay if I asked for a poem and the spirit world gave me a poem. It was okay if they used an example of things going on in my life as an analogy in their beautiful prose or to make a point during a channeling session. Hadn't they told us in poem after poem that all was One? Consciousness was consciousness. In the final analysis, there was only One Mind.

Do you see how it heals? they asked, and my answer was yes. I saw it all clearly now. My personal healing began the day Susan came back to us through the mouth of a medium. I made it my mission then and there to share the healing messages of mediumship with those in need of comfort—that there is no death, and we will see our loved ones again ... that life is eternal, and that how we live our lives now truly matters.

Now it was my lips and pen that the spirit world used, and my mind as well, it seemed. Whatever it took to get across their messages of hope.

I gave Rudy and Gretchen's leashes a gentle tug, and we headed for home.

Oh God in the heavens, may I know that heaven is where I sit. May I feel your presence in all that I do. May I see you in every face and every flower. May I know you in every second and every hour. May not a moment pass that I do not know that I am guided . . . never alone, but held safe in your arms, rocked like a baby, fully loved. In that knowingness, in the full security of your love and protection, may I go forth this day and create with you heaven on earth.

About Suzanne Giesemann

Author *Suzanne Giesemann* is a psychic-medium and metaphysical teacher focusing on personal excellence and spiritual growth. She is a former Navy Commander who served for twenty years, including duty as a Commanding Officer, Special Assistant to the Chief of Naval Operations, and Aide to the Chairman of the Joint Chiefs of Staff.

Suzanne has traveled to 54 countries and all 50 states. An avid adventurer, she and her husband, Ty, sailed their 46-foot sloop across the Atlantic Ocean to Turkey. She now dedicates her time to sharing the comforting message of mediumship with the widest possible audience.

Suzanne shares spirit-inspired messages from her daily meditations on her blog, www.SanayaSays.com. Read her spirit-inspired poetry at www.MessagesOfHopePoems.org.

Visit www.SuzanneGiesemann.com to learn more about Suzanne.

CPSIA information can be obtained at www.ICGtesting.com
Printed in the USA
LVOW13s1216260514

387236LV00005B/560/P